WORK, TRADE & FARMING
through the ages

Series Editor Dr. John Haywood

LORENZ BOOKS

First published by Lorenz Books in 2001

© Anness Publishing Limited 2001

Published in the USA by Lorenz Books, Anness Publishing Inc., 27 West 20th Street, New York NY 10011

Lorenz Books is an imprint of Anness Publishing Inc.

www.lorenzbooks.com

All rights reserved. No part of this publication may be reproduced, stored in a retrieval system, or transmitted in any way or by any means, electronic, mechanical, photocopying, recording, or otherwise, without the prior written permission of the copyright holder.

Publisher Joanna Lorenz
Managing Editor, Children's Books Gilly Cameron Cooper
Project Editor Rasha Elsaeed
Editorial Reader Joy Wotton
"From Survival to Specialization" Introduction by Fiona Macdonald
Authors Daud Ali, Jen Green, Charlotte Hurdman, Fiona Macdonald, Lorna Oakes, Philip Steele, Michael Stotter, Richard Tames
Consultants Nick Allen, Cherry Alexander, Clara Bezanilla, Felicity Cobbing, Penny Dransart, Jenny Hall, Dr John Haywood, Dr Robin Holgate, Michael Johnson, Lloyd Laing, Jessie Lim, Heidi Potter, Louise Schofield, Leslie Webster,
Designers Simon Borrough, Matthew Cook, Joyce Mason, Caroline Reeves, Margaret Sadler, Alison Walker, Stuart Watkinson at Ideas Into Print, Sarah Williams
Special Photography John Freeman
Stylists Konika Shakar, Thomasina Smith, Melanie Williams

Previously published as part of the *Step Into* series in 14 separate volumes:
Ancient Egypt, Ancient Greece, Ancient India, Ancient Japan, Arctic World, Aztec & Maya Worlds, Celtic World, Chinese Empire, Inca World, Mesopotamia, North American Indians, Roman Empire, Viking World, The Stone Age.

PICTURE CREDITS
b=bottom, t=top, c=center, l=left, r=right

Lesley & Roy Adkins Picture Library: 45b; AKG: 14t, 15tr, 46bl; B & C Alexander: 13tl, 54tr, 55tr; The Ancient Art & Architecture Collection Ltd: back cover, 2, 18t, 19t, 20l & 20r, 21l, 25tl & 25br, 32bl, 38cr, 39br, 40bl, 41cl, 42c, 43tr; E T Archives: 26br, 27tr, 29tr, 31bl & 31tr, 33tl, 37tr, 56tl & 56bl, 57br; GDR Barnett Images: 36tl, 37bl; The Bridgeman Art Library: 25tl, 27bl, 34tl, 35tl; The British Museum: 9t, 17bc, 18bl, 21br; Peter Clayton: 17bl & 17br, 18br, 21bl, 22t, 38tl, 44tl; Bruce Coleman: 8br, 9ct, 27br, 61cl; Corbis: 32br, 33b, 52t; Sue Cunningham Photographic: 60cl, 61tl & 61tr; C M Dixon: front cover, 8tl, 12bl, 16t, 17t, 23tl, 24bl, 26tl, 27bl, 29tl, 32tl, 39tl, 47tr, 40tr & 40br, 41bl, 44tr & 44b, 45t & 45c, 48tl, 49bl, 52tl; Ecoscene: 12tl; Mary Evans Picture Library: 28br, 31tl, 40cl, 54b, 55tl; FLPA: 9br, 29cr & 29br; Fortean Picture Library: 13tl; Werner Forman Archives: 31cl & 31tr, 46bl & 46bl, 48bl & 48bc, 50tl, 58tl; Robert Harding: 14b; Michael Holford: 23bl, 28tl, 41tr; The Hutchinson Library: 34cr; MacQuitty Collection: 27tl, 29bl; Museum of London: 8bl; National Museum of Copenhagen: 50cl; Peter Newark: 52tr, 53br; NHPA: 12bl; John Oakes: 15bl; Bob Partridge & the Ancient Egypt Library: 21tr; Ann & Bury Peerless: 33c; Planet Earth Pictures: 57cr; Ann Ronan: 55cl; Royal Asiatic Society: 35c; Science & Society: 54cr; Scotland in Focus: 47tl; Skyscan: 47br; South American Photo Library: 36b, 56r, 58tl, 60tr; V & A Picture Library: 35cl; Visual Arts Library: 24tl & 24c, 30cl; Wilderness Photo Library: 13bl; York Archeological Trust: 50cl, 51bc

10 9 8 7 6 5 4 3 2 1

CONTENTS

FROM SURVIVAL TO SPECIALIZATION 4

Crops in the Stone Age 8

    Taming Animals 10

    Stone Age Exchange 12

    Mesopotamian Trade Network .. 14

    Egyptian Slaves 16

Along the Banks of the Egyptian Nile 18

Skilled Workers in Egypt 20

Egyptian Trade 22

Chinese Merchants and Peasants 24

Working the Land in China 26

Chinese Silk Production 28

Coins and Markets in China 30

Money and Trade in India 32

Textiles Industry in India 34

Japanese Peasant Farmers 36

Poor Soil and Hot Sun in Greece .. 38

Seafaring Greeks 40

Ancient Greek Workshops .. 42

Shopping Roman Style 44

Celtic Farmers of Europe 46

Celtic Trade Routes 48

Long-Distance Trading in Viking Times 50

North American Trading 52

Arctic Trapping and Trade 54

Reclaiming Land in Mesoamerica 56

The Mesoamerican Market 58

Inca Master Masons 60

Glossary 62

Index 64

KEY
Look for the border patterns used throughout this book. There is one for each culture.

The Stone Age	Japan	North American Indians
Mesopotamia	Ancient Greece	
Ancient Egypt	Roman Empire	The Arctic
India	The Celts	Aztec & Maya
China	The Vikings	Inca Empire

From Survival to Specialization

Our ancestors, the first humans, survived by hunting animals and gathering wild food for almost half a million years. They lived mostly as nomads, moving from place to place according to the season. They followed herds of animals or shoals of fish, and gathered nuts, berries, and other wild plants. Their job was to survive—to find food, make tools, and build shelters. They traded with other traveling people they encountered, by exchanging useful goods they had for food, weapons and jewelry that they wanted or needed.

Around 12,000 B.C., the lifestyles of some hunter-gatherer communities began to change. They started to build permanent settlements close to reliable water supplies, to plant and harvest crops, and to domesticate (tame and use) animals. This change happened in different ways and at different times, from one part of the world to the other, depending on climate change and the local environment. By around 5000 B.C., there were farmers in almost every inhabited continent.

The development of farming

For early farmers, farming was difficult, back-breaking work. There were only stone and wood tools to work the soil. Seeds were scattered by hand.

The wild auroch was the ancestor of early farm cattle. Bones found by archaeologists show that early domesticated cattle were smaller than their wild relatives.

Timeline 100,000–550 B.C.

100,000 B.C. Peoples in many different regions of the world live as hunter-gatherers.

9000 B.C. Horses become extinct in America through over-hunting. They were reintroduced by European settlers in the A.D. 1500s.

Early people lived as hunter-gatherers

8500 B.C. Sheep and goats are domesticated in Mesopotamia (modern Iraq).

Sheep

8000 B.C. The first farming villages are built in the Middle East. Long-distance trade routes develop in Europe and the Middle East.

6300 B.C. Potatoes are cultivated in the Andes mountains of South America.

5000 B.C. Rice is cultivated in China and Southeast Asia.

4000 B.C. Wild horses are first domesticated in Russia.

3000 B.C. Corn is cultivated in Mesoamerica (Central America).

Corn

100,000 B.C.   8500 B.C.   5000 B.C.   3000

4 INTRODUCTION

has been called a revolution, because it dramatically changed how people lived and worked. Until the 1700s, most people around the world were farmers in settled villages, or they found work connected with growing crops, raising animals or transporting and processing food. In different civilizations, farmwork was organized in many different ways. Sometimes farmworkers were peasants, working for just themselves and their families. In other parts of the world, such as in Celtic Europe, ancient China, and Egypt, the land was owned by a lord, and workers had to pay him service and loyalty. In ancient Egypt, Greece, and Rome, these workers were often unpaid slaves.

Not everyone made their living from the land. Permanent settlements (that is, villages and later, towns) also became centers for crafts, trade, and building work. Men and women survived by using special skills such as stonemasonry, carving, working with clay, metal and textiles, or by buying and selling goods made by others. Some cultures specialized in particular work. Remains of grand temples in Egypt and Central

When people figured out how to cultivate the waterlogged fields of China and Southeast Asia, rice became the main crop of these areas.

This Mesopotamian clay figure of a woman holding a baby dates from c.5500 B.C. At this time, towns were growing into cities, and craftspeople were becoming more skilled.

2600 B.C. In Europe, farmers invent tools and techniques to increase production, including milking cattle, riding horses, cultivating fields with ox-drawn plows, and using shears to cut the wool from sheep.

Ox-drawn plows

2000 B.C. Egyptian and Mesopotamian merchants travel by land and sea to trade in luxury goods.

1500 B.C. The shaduf (way of lifting water to irrigate fields) was brought to Egypt from the Middle East. It helped Egyptian farmers grow bigger crops by making better use of the Nile floods.

900 B.C. Mayan farmers in Central America build irrigation systems to water their fields.

750 B.C. The first Chinese coins were made.

750–550 B.C. Greek farmers set up colonies in lands around the Mediterranean Sea.

A trader's pair of scales

2000 B.C.   750 B.C.   550 B.C.

FROM SURVIVAL TO SPECIALIZATION 5

Tomb paintings tell us a lot about life in ancient Egypt. This painting shows how building bricks were made—by mixing clay and straw in a big, rotating pot.

America, and public buildings in Peru, show that people in those areas were expert stonemasons, even though their tools were basic. The ancient Greeks, Romans, Celts, and Vikings produced many fine objects of art, including pottery, jewelry and sculptures. These were often made by craftspeople in workshops in towns.

Qin Shi Huangdi (the first Emperor in China) introduced round coins with holes. People could carry them easily on a string.

Some regions specialized in making or trading in valuable items. Silk came from China, spices from India and Southeast Asia, gold from Africa, and perfumes from Arabia. Goods made or processed in villages were offered for sale at local markets. The finest products were often transported to sell in distant lands. At first, they were bartered (exchanged for other items of equal value). Business deals became much easier after coins were invented—in China around 750 B.C. and in Lydia (modern Turkey) around 600 B.C.

Many towns on trading routes grew into powerful cities and became centers of organized government and trade. They were places where rulers lived, surrounded by people such as

Women often had the job of going to the market. Here, one Aztec woman in Tlatelolco is selling corn to another.

Timeline 635 B.C.–A.D. 1900

635 B.C. The first coins in Europe were made in Lydia (modern Turkey).

*c.*400–300 B.C. Celtic Europe prospers. Farmers build round-house villages. Celtic traders travel long distances to trade with the merchants from Rome and Greece. After around 200 B.C., the Celts build *oppida* (fortified towns) to trade.

*c.*110 B.C. Trade begins between China, Central Asia, the Middle East and Europe along the Silk Road.

A.D. 50 Roman traders reach India and Bengal.

A.D. 200 The Hopewell people of North America set up trade routes.

A.D. 250–900 The Maya prosper. Farmers grow corn, beans, squash, cacao and tropical fruits in slash-and-burn fields.

A.D. 300 Tea is first cultivated in China.

A brazier (used to hold hot coal) made in Baghdad c.A.D. 800, was probably brought by a Viking merchant to Scandinavia

A.D. 750–1100 Vikings from northern Europe establish trade with merchants from the Middle East.

1325 The Aztecs of Mexico build a new capital city in the middle of a lake. They

635 B.C.   A.D. 50   A.D. 750   1325

servants, stonemasons, scribes, lawyers, soldiers, and officials.

As towns grew bigger and more complex, so did people's needs. They wanted comfortable homes, public buildings and good roads, as well as teachers, doctors, and priests to tend to their physical, mental and spiritual wellbeing. Over time, craftsmen, artists, and entertainers came to live and work in towns. The large numbers of people living there meant that they would find willing audiences and rich patrons to support them financially.

As towns grew into trading centers, rulers became responsible for governing the people and providing safe passage for merchants. Mesopotamian kings were often surrounded by other nobles, who helped with running their empire, or celebrating a successful bull hunt!

In this thematic history, you can compare how different working activities, from farming and building to textile production and crafts, developed in different civilizations through time. You will be able to see which regions became known for particular industries, and how trading links were first established between the Americas, Europe, the Middle East, and Southeast Asia.

Mesoamerican featherworkers wove feathers to make shields, headdresses, cloaks, and fans. Mesoamerican crafts were known for their beautiful designs.

surround it with *chinampas* (market-gardens) where they grow fruit, vegetables and flowers.

1475 The Aztecs conquer the trading city of Tlatelolco, and make it the greatest market in Central America.

1540 The first European traders and missionaries arrive in Japan. European traders hope to find spices and rich silks. Missionaries want to spread the Christian faith throughout Japan.

1603 A long period of peace in Japan. Trade and towns expand, and new forms of art and entertainment, such as *kabuki* plays, develop.

Portuguese sailor

1700–1900 European whaling expeditions and trading companies introduce great changes to traditional life for many people in the Arctic.

Whale hunting in the Arctic

FROM SURVIVAL TO SPECIALIZATION 7

Crops in the Stone Age

IN ABOUT 8000 B.C., people in the Near East began growing their own food for the first time. Instead of gathering and eating the seeds of wild grasses, such as wheat and barley, they saved some of it. Then, the following year, they planted it to produce a crop. As they began to control their food sources, the first farmers found that a small area of land could now feed a much larger population. People began living in permanent settlements, in order to tend their crops and guard their harvest. Over the next 5000 years, farming spread from the Near East to western Asia, Europe, and Africa. Farming also developed separately in other parts of Asia around 6500 B.C. and in America by about 7000 B.C.

The first farms were in hill country where wheat and barley grew naturally and there was enough rain for crops to grow. As populations increased, villages began to appear along river valleys, where farmers could water their crops at dry times of the year.

STONE TOOLS
This chipped flint is the blade of a hoe. It was used in North America between about A.D. 900 and A.D. 1200, but it is very similar to the hoes used by the first farmers to break up the soil. Rakes made from deer antlers were used to cover the seeds. Ripe corn was harvested with sharp flint sickle blades.

SICKLE BLADE
Ears of ripe corn would either have been plucked by hand or harvested with sickles such as this flint sickle. The blade has been hafted, or inserted, into a modern wooden handle.

WILD RICE
Rice is a type of grass that grows in hot, damp areas, such as swamps. It was a good food source for early hunter-gatherers along rivers and coasts in southern Asia. The seeds were collected when ripe, and stored for use when little other food was available. The grain could be kept for many months.

World Crops

The first plants in the world to be domesticated, or farmed, were those that grew naturally in an area. Wheat and barley grew wild in the Near East. In India, China, and Southeast Asia, rice was domesticated by 5000 B.C. and soon became the main food crop. Around 3000 B.C. in Mexico, farmers grew corn, beans, and squash. Further south in the Andes mountains, the chief crops were potatoes, sweet potatoes, and corn.

corn   *butternut squash*

Grinding Grain

This stone quern, or hand-mill, is 6000 years old. It was used to grind grain into coarse flour for making porridge or bread. The grain was placed on the flat stone and ground into flour with the smooth, heavy, rubbing stone. Flour that was made this way often contained a lot of grit. To make bread, water was added to the flour. The dough was then shaped into flat loaves, which were baked in a clay oven.

Straight Track

Several tracks were built across marshes between 4000 and 2000 B.C. in southern England. In some cases, these were used to link settlements to nearby fields of crops. The long, thin rods used to build the track above tell us a lot about the surrounding woodlands. The trees were coppiced, which means that the thin shoots growing from cut hazel trees were harvested every few years.

A Step Up

These terraced hillsides are in the Andes mountains of Peru. In mountainous areas where rainfall was high, some early farmers began cutting terraces, or steps, into the steep hillsides. The terraces meant that every scrap of soil could be used for planting. They prevented soil from eroding, or washing away. Farmers also used terracing to control the irrigation, or watering, of their crops. One of the first crops to be cultivated in Peru was the potato, which can be successfully grown high above sea level.

CROPS IN THE STONE AGE   9

Taming Animals

About the same time that people began to grow crops, they also started to domesticate (tame) wild animals. Wild sheep, goats, pigs, and cattle had been hunted for thousands of years before people started to round them up into pens. Hunters may have done this to make the animals easier to catch. These animals gradually got used to people and became tamer. The first animals to be kept like this were probably sheep and goats around 8500 B.C. in the Near East.

Herders soon noticed that larger animals often had larger young. They began to allow only the finest animals to breed, so that domestic animals gradually became much stronger and larger than wild ones. As well as four-legged livestock, chickens were domesticated for their eggs and meat. In South America, the llama was kept for its meat and wool, along with ducks and guinea pigs. In Southeast Asia, pigs were the most important domestic animals.

Wild Cattle
This bull is an aurochs, or wild ox. The aurochs was the ancestor of today's domestic cattle. Taming these huge, fierce animals was much harder than keeping sheep and goats. Wild cattle were probably not tamed until about 7000 B.C. The aurochs became extinct in A.D. 1627. In the 1930s, a German biologist recreated the animal by crossing domesticated breeds such as Friesians and Highland cattle.

Wild Horses
Horses were a favorite food for prehistoric hunter-gatherers. This sculpture of a wild horse was found in Germany. It was made around 4000 B.C. Horses also often appear in cave art. They were probably first domesticated in Russia around 4400 B.C. In America, horses had become extinct through over-hunting by 9000 B.C. They were reintroduced by European explorers in the A.D. 1500s.

10 The Stone Age 120,000 B.C.–2000 B.C.

Dingoes and Dogs

The dingo is the wild dog of Australia. It is the descendant of tame dogs that were brought to the country more than 10,000 years ago by Aboriginal Australians. Dogs were probably the first animals to be domesticated. Their wolf ancestors were tamed to help with hunting, and later, with herding and guarding. In North America, dogs were used as pack animals and dragged a travois (sled) behind them.

Desert Herders

Small herds of wild cattle were probably first domesticated in the Sahara and the Near East. This rock painting comes from the Tassili n'Ajjer area of the Sahara Desert. It was painted in about 6000 B.C., at a time when much of the Sahara was covered by grassland and shallow lakes. The painting shows a group of herders with their cattle outside a plan of their house.

Llamas

The llama was domesticated in central Peru by 3500 B.C. It was kept first for its meat and wool, but later it was also used for carrying food and goods long distances. A relative of the llama, the alpaca, was also domesticated for its wool.

Goats and Sheep

Rock paintings in the Sahara show goats and sheep, among the first animals to be domesticated. They were kept for their meat, milk, hides, and wool, and are still some of the most common farm animals.

TAMING ANIMALS 11

Stone Age Exchange

COWRIE SHELLS
Small, highly polished cowrie shells were popular as decoration for clothes and jewelry in prehistoric times. The shells have been found scattered around skeletons in burial sites, many of which are hundreds of miles from the coast. Later, cowrie shells were used as money in Africa and parts of Asia.

STONE AGE PEOPLE did not use banknotes and coins for money, as we do. Instead they bartered, or exchanged, things. When one person wanted a bowl, for example, he or she had to offer something in exchange to the owner of the bowl—perhaps a tool or ornament. Toward the end of the Stone Age, however, people began to use shells or stone rings as a kind of currency.

Even isolated hunter-gatherer groups came into contact with each other and exchanged things, such as seashells, for tools or hides. With the beginning of farming around 8000 B.C. in the Near East, however, long-distance exchange and a more organized trading system began. New activities, such as farming, pottery, and weaving, needed specialized tools, so a high value was put on suitable rocks. In western Europe, flint mines and stone quarries produced ax blades that were prized and traded over great distances. Sometimes goods were traded thousands of miles from where they were made.

AXES
A good, strong ax was a valuable commodity. It was particularly important for early farmers, who used it to chop down trees and clear land for crops. Ax heads made of special stone were traded across wide distances.

BURIED WITH WEALTH
This communal burial on the Solomon Islands in the Pacific Ocean shows the deceased accompanied by shells and ornaments. Shells have been used for money for thousands of years—in fact, for longer and over a wider area than any currency including coins. One hoard of shells, found in Iraq, was dated to earlier than 18,000 B.C.

STONE TRADE
During the neolithic period there was a widespread trade in stone for axes. At Graig in Clwyd, Wales (*left*), stone was quarried from the scree slopes and taken all over Britain. The blades were roughly cut on site, then transported to other parts of the country, where they were ground and polished into ax heads. Rough, unfinished axes have been found lying on the ground at Graig.

FUR TRAPPER
A modern Cree trapper from the Canadian Arctic is surrounded by his catch of pine marten pelts. Furs were almost definitely a valuable commodity for prehistoric peoples, especially for hunter-gatherers who traded with more settled farmers. They could be traded for food or precious items, such as amber or tools.

SKINS AND PELTS
White arctic fox skins are left to dry in the cold air. In the winter, arctic foxes grow a thick white coat so that they are well camouflaged against the snow. Furs like this have traditionally been particularly valuable to arctic peoples, both for the clothing that makes arctic life possible, and for trading.

Mesopotamian Trade Network

THE PEOPLE OF MESOPOTAMIA (present-day Iraq) were very enterprising and expert business people. They traveled long distances to obtain goods they needed, and imported timber, meta, and semiprecious stones.

Around 2000 B.C., the Assyrians had a widespread, long-distance trading network in Anatolia (modern Turkey). The headquarters were in the northern Mesopotamian city of Ashur, and the trade was controlled by the city government and by large family firms.

The head of a firm usually stayed in Ashur, but trusted members of the family were based in Anatolian cities such as Kanesh. From here, they conducted business on the firm's behalf, going on business trips around Anatolia, and collecting debts and interest on loans. Deals were made on a credit basis—for the Assyrian families acted as money-lenders and bankers as well. At the point of delivery, goods and transportation (the donkeys) were exchanged for silver, which was then sent back to Ashur. In about 2000 B.C., one Kanesh businessman failed to return the silver, and the company threatened to send for the police.

TROPHIES AND TAXES
Carved ivory furniture and bronze bowls were often plundered after successful battles. There is little evidence of trade in Mesopotamia from 900 to 600 B.C. The Assyrian kings helped themselves to anything they wanted from the people they defeated. They collected as taxes whatever was needed, such as straw and fodder for horses.

TRADE TO KANESH
Donkeys and mules are still used to transport goods from one village to another in modern Iraq. When trade with ancient Turkey was at its peak, donkey caravans took large amounts of tin and textiles through the mountain passes to Kanesh. A typical load for one donkey would usually consist of 130 minas (about 145 pounds) of tin (which was specially packed and sealed by the city authorities) and ten pieces of woolen cloth.

PRECIOUS THINGS

The marvelous jewelry in the Royal Graves of Ur not only demonstrates the skills of the jewelers who made it, but is also evidence that the Sumerians engaged in long-distance trade. None of the materials used to make the jewelry was available in Sumer, so precious stones had to be imported. The gold may have come from Oman, the lapis lazuli from Afghanistan, and the semiprecious stones from the Indus Valley.

semiprecious stones

lapis lazuli

gold

STRIKING A DEAL

Two merchants make a contract. One is agreeing to supply goods for a certain amount of silver, and the other is promising to pay by a certain date. The details of a deal were written on a clay tablet and impressed with the cylinder seals of the two men. Often a copy was made and put in a clay envelope. If there was a dispute about the deal later, the envelope would be broken and the agreement checked.

LETTERS FROM KANESH

The site of the trading settlement of Kanesh, where the Assyrians did an enormous amount of business, has been excavated. A large number of clay tablets have been found, many of them business letters. From these letters, it is clear that the Anatolian princes had the first choice of the goods brought by Assyrian merchants. They charged the merchants taxes on their donkey caravans. In return, the princes protected the roads and provided insurance against robbers.

CASH AND CARRY

There was no money in Mesopotamia, so goods were usually paid for in silver. Silver was measured in shekels and each shekel weighed about ⅓ ounce. It was carefully weighed to make sure that the person who was paying gave an amount equal to the value of the goods that he or she was buying.

Egyptian Slaves

THE PHARAOHS may have believed that it was their links with the gods that kept Egypt going, but really it was the hard work of the ordinary people. It was they who dug the soil, worked in the mines and quarries, sailed the boats on the river Nile, marched with the army into Syria or Nubia, cooked food, and raised children.

Slavery was not very important in ancient Egypt, but it did exist. Most of the slaves were prisoners who had been captured during the many wars that Egypt fought with their neighbors in the Near East. Slaves were usually treated well and were allowed to own property.

Many Egyptian workers were serfs. This meant that their freedom was limited. They could be bought and sold along with the estates where they worked. Farmers had to be registered with the government. They had to sell crops at a fixed price and pay taxes in the form of produce. During the season of the Nile floods, when the fields lay under water, many workers were recruited into public building projects. Punishment for those who ran away was harsh.

PLOWING WITH OXEN
A model figure from a tomb shows a farmer plowing the soil with oxen. The Egyptian farm workers' daily toil was hard. Unskilled peasant laborers did not own land and were paid little.

TRANSPORTING A STATUE
These workers are moving a huge stone statue on a wooden sled hauled by ropes. Many farm workers had to labor on large public building works, building dams or pyramids, each summer and autumn. Their food and lodging were provided, but they were not paid wages. Only the official classes were exempt from this service, but anyone rich enough could pay someone else to do the work for them. Slaves were used for really hard labor, such as mining and quarrying.

COUNTING GEESE
A farmer's flock of geese is counted in this wall painting. Every other year, government officials visited each farm. They would count the animals to see how much tax had to be paid to the pharaoh. Taxes were paid in produce rather than money. The scribe on the left is recording this information. Scribes were members of the official classes and therefore had a higher position than other workers.

CARRYING BREAD
A woman carries a tray of loaves on her head. Most of the cooking in large houses and palaces was done by male servants, but baking bread was the job of the women. Baking was one of the few public jobs open to women.

GRINDING CORN
This model from 2325 B.C. shows a female servant grinding wheat or barley grains into flour. She is using a stone hand-mill called a quern.

GIVE THAT MAN A BEATING
In this tomb painting, an official is shown overseeing work in the fields. Unskilled peasant farmers were attached to an estate belonging to the pharaoh, a temple, or a rich landowner. Farmers who could not, or would not, give a large percentage of their harvest in rent and taxes to the pharaoh were punished harshly. They might be beaten, and their tools or their house could be seized as payment. There were law courts, judges, and local magistrates in place to punish tax collectors who took bribes.

EGYPTIAN SLAVES

Along the Banks of the Egyptian Nile

THE ANCIENT EGYPTIANS called the banks of the Nile "the Black Land," because of the mud that was washed downstream each year from Africa. The Nile flooded in June, depositing this rich, fertile mud along its valley in Egypt. The land remained underwater until autumn.

By November, the ground was ready for plowing and then sowing. Seeds were scattered on the soil and trampled in by sheep or goats. During drier periods of the year, farmers dug channels and canals to bring water from the river to irrigate their land. In the New Kingdom (1550 B.C.–1070 B.C.), a lifting system called the shaduf was introduced to raise water from the river. The success of the farming cycle was vital. Years of low flood or drought could spell disaster. If the crops failed, people went hungry.

Farm animals included ducks, geese, pigs, sheep, and goats. Cows grazed the fringes of the desert and the greener lands of the delta region, north of Egypt. Oxen were used for hauling plows and donkeys for carrying goods.

HARVEST FESTIVAL
A priestess makes an offering of harvest produce in the tomb of Nakht. The picture shows some of the delicious fruits grown in ancient Egypt. These included figs, grapes, and pomegranates.

FARMING TOOLS
Hoes were used to break up soil that had been too heavy for the plows. They were also used for digging soil. The sharp sickle was used to cut grain.

sickle   *hoes*

TOILING IN THE FIELDS
Grain crops were usually harvested in March or April, before the great heat began. The ears of wheat and barley were cut off with a sickle made of wood and sharpened flint. In some well-irrigated areas, there was a second harvest in the late summer

MAKE A SHADUF

You will need: card, pencil, ruler, scissors, glue, masking tape, acrylic paint (blue, green, brown), water pot and brush, balsa wood strips, small stones, twig, clay, hessian, string.
Note: mix green paint with dried herbs for the grass mixture.

Cut out the cardboard shapes (a), (b), and (c) as shown.

a = irrigation channel & river bank
b = river
c = water tank

1 Glue the edges of boxes (a), (b), and (c), as shown. Bind them with masking tape until they are dry. Paint the river (b) and the water tank (c) blue; allow to dry.

18 ANCIENT EGYPT 6000 B.C.–50 B.C.

HERDING THE OXEN
This New Kingdom wall painting shows oxen being herded in front of a government inspector. Cattle were already being bred along the banks of the Nile in the days before the pharaohs. They provided milk, meat, and leather. They hauled wooden plows, and were killed as sacrifices to the gods in the temples.

NILE CROPS
The chief crops were barley and wheat, used for making beer and bread. Beans and lentils were grown next to leeks, onions, cabbages, radishes, lettuces, and cucumbers. Juicy melons, dates, and figs could be grown in desert oases. Grapes were grown in vineyards.

leeks   *onions*

WATERING MACHINE
The shaduf has a bucket on one end of a pole and a heavy weight at the other. First the weight is pushed up, lowering the bucket into the river. As the weight is lowered, it raises up the full bucket.

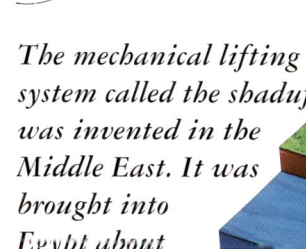

The mechanical lifting system called the shaduf was invented in the Middle East. It was brought into Egypt about 3,500 years ago.

2 Paint the river bank with the green grass mixture on top, brown on the sides, and the irrigation channel blue. Next, get the balsa strips for the frame of the shaduf.

3 Glue the strips together, supporting them with masking tape and a piece of card. When dry, paint the frame brown. Glue the stones on the water tank.

4 Use a twig for the shaduf pole. Make a weight from clay wrapped in hessian. Tie it to one end of the pole. Make a bucket from clay, leaving two holes for the string.

5 Thread the string through the bucket and tie to the pole. Tie the pole, with its weight and bucket, to the shaduf frame. Finally, glue the frame to the bank.

ALONG THE BANKS OF THE EGYPTIAN NILE   19

Skilled Workers in Egypt

In ancient Egypt, skilled workers formed a middle class between the poor laborers, and the rich officials and nobles. Wall paintings and models show us craftspeople carving stone or wood, making pottery, and working precious metals. There were boat builders and chariot makers, too.

Artists and craftspeople could be well rewarded for their skills, and some became famous for their work. The house and workshops of a sculptor called Thutmose was excavated in el-Amarna in 1912. He was very successful in his career, and was a favorite of the royal family.

Craftspeople often lived in their own part of town. A special village was built at Deir el-Medina, near Thebes, for the builders of the magnificent, but secret, royal tombs. Among the 100 or so houses there, archaeologists found delivery notes for goods, sketches and plans drawn on broken pottery. Sometimes working conditions may not have been very good—records show that the workers once went on strike, and they may well have helped to rob the tombs that they themselves had built.

GLASS IN GOLD
This pendant shows the skill of Egyptian craftspeople. It is in the form of Nekhbet the vulture, the goddess of Upper Egypt. Glass of many colors has been set in solid gold using a technique called cloisonné. Like many other such beautiful objects, it was found in the tomb of Tutankhamun.

JEWELERS AT WORK
Jewelers are shown at their work benches in this wall painting from 1395 B.C. One is making an ornamental collar, and the others are working with precious stones and beads. The bow strings are being used to power metal drill bits.

A Hive of Industry
Skilled craftsmen are hard at work in this bustling workshop. Carpenters are sawing and drilling wood, potters are painting pottery jars, and masons are chiseling stone. A foreman would inspect the quality of each finished item.

Deir el-Medina
The stone foundations of the village of Deir el-Medina may still be seen on the west bank of the Nile. They are about 3,500 years old. In its day, Deir el-Medina housed the skilled workers who built and decorated the royal tombs in the Valley of the Kings. The men worked for eight days out of ten. The village existed for four centuries, and was large and prosperous. Nevertheless, the workmen's village did not have its own water supply, so water had to be carried to the site and stored in a guarded tank.

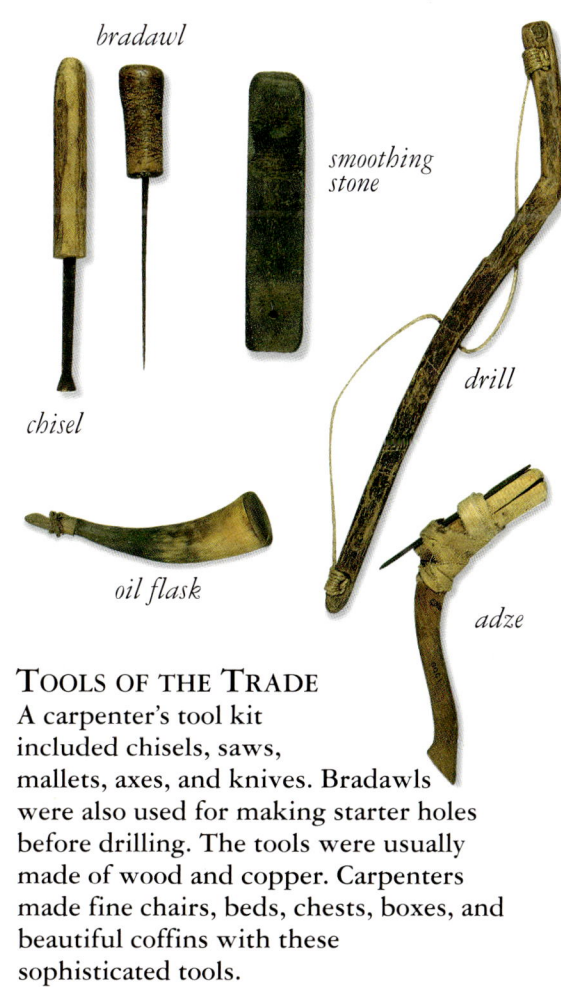

bow drill, *bradawl*, *chisel*, *smoothing stone*, *drill*, *oil flask*, *adze*, *saw*, *axe*, *pull saw*

Surveying the Land
Officials stretch a cord across a field to calculate its area. These men have been employed to survey an estate for government records.

Tools of the Trade
A carpenter's tool kit included chisels, saws, mallets, axes, and knives. Bradawls were also used for making starter holes before drilling. The tools were usually made of wood and copper. Carpenters made fine chairs, beds, chests, boxes, and beautiful coffins with these sophisticated tools.

SKILLED WORKERS IN EGYPT

Egyptian Trade

AT ITS HEIGHT, the Egyptian Empire stretched all the way from Nubia, in southern Egypt, to Syria on the Mediterranean coast. The peoples of the Near East who were conquered had to pay tribute to the pharaohs in the form of valuable goods such as gold or ostrich feathers. However, the Egyptians were more interested in protecting their own land from invasion than in establishing a huge empire. They preferred to conquer by influence rather than by war. Egyptian trading influence spread far and wide as official missions set out to find luxury goods for the pharaoh and his court—timber, precious stones, and spices. Beautiful pottery was imported from the Minoan kingdom of Crete. Traders employed by the government were called shwty. The ancient Egyptians did not have coins, and so goods were exchanged in a system of bartering.

Expeditions also set out to the land of Punt, probably a part of east Africa. The traders brought back pet apes, greyhounds, gold, ivory, ebony, and myrrh. The Egyptian queen, Hatshepsut, encouraged these trading expeditions. The walls of her mortuary temple record details of them, and also show a picture of Eti, the Queen of Punt.

WOODS FROM FARAWAY FORESTS
Few trees grew in Egypt, so timber for making fine furniture had to be imported. Cedarwood came from Lebanon, and hardwoods, such as ebony, from Africa.

ALL THE RICHES OF PUNT
Sailors load a wooden sailing boat with storage jars, plants, spices, and apes from the land of Punt. Goods would have been exchanged in Punt for these items. Egyptian trading expeditions traveled to many distant lands and brought back precious goods to the pharaoh. This drawing is copied from the walls of Hatshepsut's temple at Deir el-Bahri.

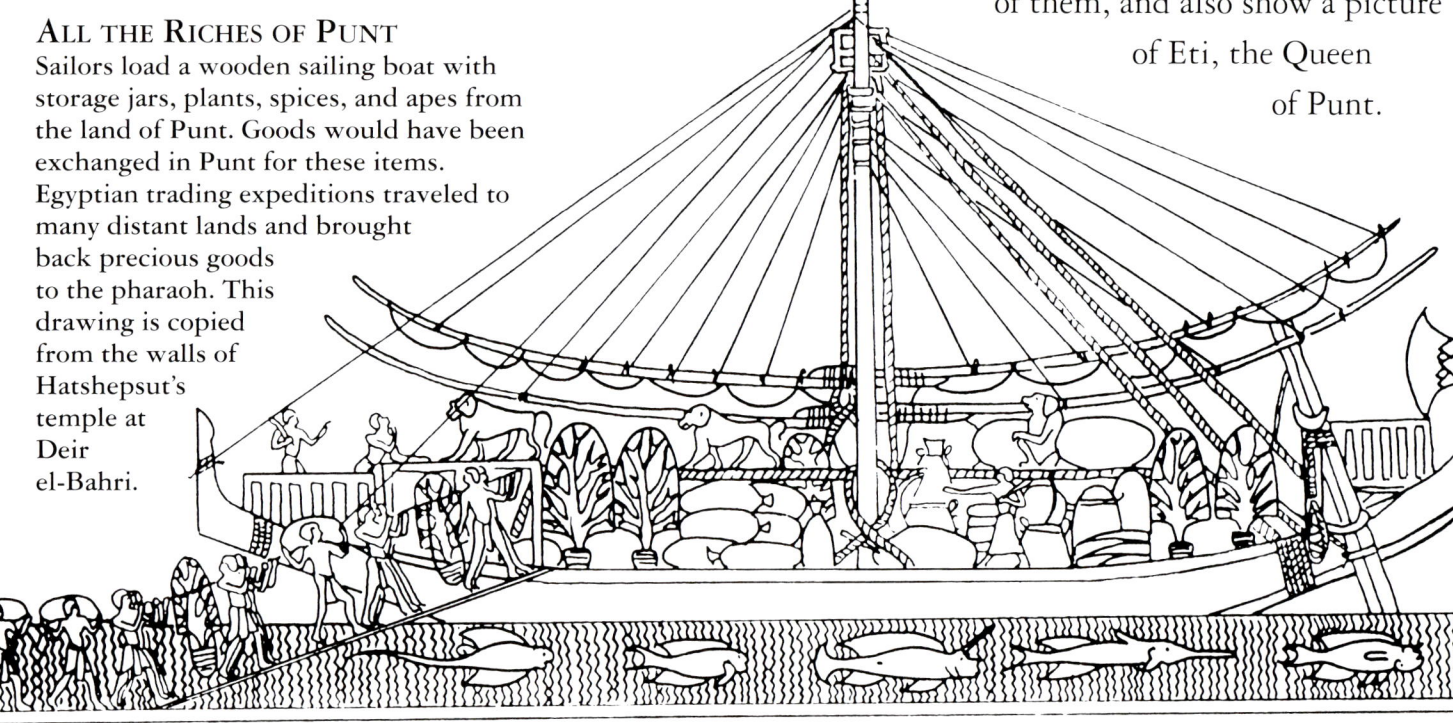

SYRIAN ENVOYS
Foreign rulers from Asia and the Mediterranean lands would send splendid gifts to the pharaoh, and he would send them gifts in return. These Syrians have been sent as representatives of their ruler, or envoys. They have brought perfume containers made of gold, ivory, and a beautiful stone called lapis lazuli. The vases are decorated with gold and lotus flower designs. The pharaoh would pass on some of the luxurious foreign gifts to his favorite courtiers.

NUBIANS BRINGING TRIBUTE
Nubians bring goods to the pharaoh Thutmose IV—gold rings, apes, and leopard skins. Nubia was the land above the Nile cataracts (rapids), now known as northern Sudan. The Egyptians acquired much of their wealth from Nubia through military campaigns. During times of peace, however, they also traded with the princes of Nubia for minerals and exotic animals.

EXOTIC GOODS
Egyptian craftsmen had to import many of their most valuable materials from abroad. These included gold, elephant tusks (for ivory), hardwoods, such as ebony, and softwoods, such as cedar of Lebanon. Copper was mined in Nubia, and bronze (a mixture of copper and tin) was imported from Syria.

ivory *ebony*

A WORLD OF TRADE
The Egyptians traveled over the Red Sea to the mysterious land of Punt. This modern map shows the voyage the traders would have made. No one is sure of the exact location of Punt, but it was probably either present-day Somalia, Eritrea, Yemen, or southern Sudan.

EGYPTIAN TRADE

Chinese Merchants and Peasants

THE RIVER VALLEYS AND COASTS of China have always been among the most crowded places on earth. The thinker, Confucius, with his love of social order, had taught that this vast society could be divided into four main groups. At the top were the nobles, the scholars, and the landowners. Next came the farmers, including even the poorest peasants. These people were valued because they worked for the good of the whole nation, providing the vast amounts of food necessary to feed an ever-increasing population. In third place were the skilled workers and craftspeople. In the lowest place of all were the merchants, because Confucius believed they worked for their own profit, rather than for the good of the people as a whole. However, the way in which Chinese society rewarded these groups in practice did not fit the theory. Merchants ended up becoming the richest citizens, lending money to the upper classes. In contrast, the highly valued peasants often led a dismal life, losing their homes to floods and earthquakes, or starving in years of famine.

TOP BRASS
This is what important government officials would have looked like in the early 1600s. The government employed several thousand high-ranking officials. The civil service was regarded as the most honorable and best-rewarded profession. The entry examinations were open to all men. Even the poor could rise to the ruling class if they passed the examinations.

THE IDEAL ORDER?
A government official tours the fields, where respectful peasants are happily at work. This painting shows an idealized view of the society proposed by Confucius. The district prospers and flourishes, because everybody knows their place in society. The reality was very different—while Chinese officials led comfortable lives, most people were very poor and suffered great hardship. They toiled in the fields for little reward. Officials provided aid for the victims of famine and flood, but they never tackled the injustice of the social order. Peasant uprisings were common through much of Chinese history.

Working in the Clay Pits
The manufacture of pottery was one of imperial China's most important industries. There were state-owned factories as well as many smaller private workshops. The industry employed some very highly skilled workers, and also thousands of unskilled laborers, whose job was to dig out the precious clay. They had to work very hard for little pay. Sometimes there were serious riots to demand better working conditions.

Dragon-backbone Machine
Peasants enlist the aid of machinery to help work the rice fields. The life of a peasant was mostly made up of back-breaking toil. The relentless work was made slightly easier by some clever, labor-saving inventions. The square-pallet chain pump (*shown above*) was invented in about A.D. 100. It was known as "the dragon-backbone machine," and was used to raise water to the flooded terraces where rice was grown. Men and women worked from dawn to dusk to supply food for the population.

Life Behind a Desk
Country magistrates try to remember the works of Confucius during a tough public examination. A passing grade would provide them with a path to wealth and social success. A failure would mean disgrace. The Chinese civil service was founded in about 900 B.C. This painting dates from the Qing dynasty (1644–1912). There were exams for all ranks of officials and they were very hard. The classic writings had to be remembered by heart, and so candidates sometimes cheated!

Tokens of Wealth
Merchants may have had low social status, but they had riches beyond the dreams of peasants. They accrued wealth through money-lending and by exporting luxury goods, such as silk, spices, and tea. The influence of the merchant class is reflected in the first bronze Chinese coins (*c.* 250 B.C.), which were shaped to look like knives, hoes, and spades. Merchants traded or bartered these tools.

knife

hoe

Chinese Merchants and Peasants 25

Working the Land in China

EIGHT THOUSAND YEARS AGO, most Chinese people were already living by farming. The best soil lay beside the great rivers in central and eastern China, where floods left behind rich, fertile mud. Then, as today, wheat and millet were grown in the north. This region was mostly farmed by peasants with small plots of land. Rice was cultivated in the warm, wet south, where wealthy city-dwellers owned large estates. Pears and oranges were grown in orchards.

Tea—later to become one of China's most famous exports—was first cultivated about 1,700 years ago. Hemp was also grown for its fibers, used to make coarse cloth. During the 500s B.C., cotton was introduced. Farmers raised pigs, ducks, chickens, and geese, and oxen and water buffalo were used as laboring animals on the farm. Most peasants used basic tools, such as stone hoes and wooden rakes. Plows with iron blades were used from about 600 B.C. Other inventions to help farmers were developed in the next few hundred years, including the wheelbarrow, a pedal hammer for husking grain, and a rotary winnowing fan.

PIGS ARE FARM FAVORITES
This pottery model of pigs in their sty dates back about 2,000 years. Pigs were popular farm animals, since they are easy to feed, and most parts of a pig can be eaten. They were kept in the city and also in rural country areas.

FEEDING THE MANY
Rice has been grown in the wetter regions of China since ancient times. Wheat and millet are grown in the drier regions. Sprouts of the Indian mung bean add important vitamins to many dishes.

mung beans *millet*
rice *wheat*

CHINESE TEAS
Delicate leaves of tea are picked from the bushes and gathered in large baskets on this estate in the 1800s. The Chinese cultivated tea in ancient times, but it became much more popular during the Tang dynasty (A.D. 618–906). The leaves were picked, laid out in the sun, rolled by hand, and then dried over charcoal fires.

A Helping Hand
A farmer uses a pair of strong oxen to help him plow his land. This wall painting, which was found in Jiayuguan, dates back to about 100 B.C. Oxen saved farmers a lot of time and effort. The Chinese first used oxen for farming in about 1122 B.C.

Keeping Warm
This model of a Chinese farmer's lambing shed dates from about 100 B.C., during the Han dynasty. Sheepskins were worn for warmth, but wool never became an important textile for clothes or blankets in China.

Harvesting Rice—China's Main Food
Chinese peasants pull up rice plants for threshing and winnowing in the 1600s. Farming methods were passed on by word of mouth and in handbooks from the earliest times. They advised farmers on everything from fertilizing the soil, to controlling pests.

A Timeless Scene
Peasants bend over to plant rows of rice seedlings in the flooded paddy fields of Yunnan province, in southwest China. This modern photograph is a typical scene of agricultural life in China's warm and wet southwest region. Little has changed in hundreds of years of farming.

Chinese Silk Production

For years, the Chinese tried to stop outsiders from finding out how they made their most popular export—si, or silk. The shimmering colors and smooth textures of Chinese silk made it the wonder of the ancient world. Other countries such as India discovered the secret of silk making, but China remained the producer of the world's best silk.

Silk production probably dates back to late Stone Age times (8000 B.C.–2500 B.C.) in China. Legend says that the process was invented by the empress Lei Zu in about 2640 B.C. Silkworms (the caterpillars of a type of moth) are kept on trays and fed on the leaves of white mulberry trees. The silkworms spin a cocoon (casing) of fine, but very strong, filaments. The cocoons are plunged into boiling water to separate the filaments, which are then carefully wound on to reels.

A filament of silk can be up to 1,300 yards long. Several filaments are spun together to make the thread, which is then woven into cloth on a loom. The Chinese used silk to make all kinds of beautiful products. They learned to weave flimsy gauzes and rich brocades, and they then wove elaborate colored patterns into the cloth in a style known as ke si, or cut silk.

Preparing the Thread
A young woman winds silk thread on bobbins in the late 1700s. Up to 30 filaments of silk could be twisted together to make silk thread for weaving. The Chinese made ingenious equipment for spinning silk into thread. They also built looms for weaving thread into large rolls of fabric. By the 1600s, the city of Nanjing alone had an estimated 50,000 looms.

Load those Bales!
Workers at a Chinese silk factory of the 1840s carry large bales of woven silk down to the jetty. From there the woven cloth would be shipped to the city. It might be used to make a costume for a lady of the court, or else exported abroad. The Chinese silk industry reached its peak of prosperity in the mid-1800s.

THE DRAGON ON THE EMPEROR'S BACK
A scaly red dragon writhes across a sea of yellow silk. The dragon was embroidered on a robe for an emperor of the Qing dynasty. The exquisite clothes made for the Chinese imperial court at this time are considered to be great works of art.

WINDING SILK
Silk is being prepared at this workshop of the 1600s. The workers are taking filaments (threads) from the cocoons and winding them on a reel. Traditionally, the chief areas of silk production in imperial China were in the east coast provinces of Zhejiang and Jiangsu. Silk was also produced in large quantities in Sichuan, in the west.

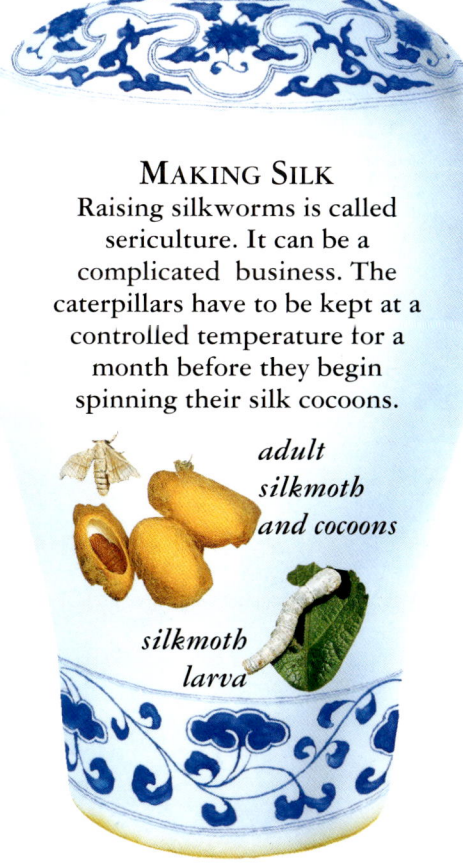

MAKING SILK
Raising silkworms is called sericulture. It can be a complicated business. The caterpillars have to be kept at a controlled temperature for a month before they begin spinning their silk cocoons.

adult silkmoth and cocoons

silkmoth larva

MAGIC MULBERRIES
These Han dynasty workers are collecting mulberry leaves in big baskets, over 2,000 years ago. These would have been used to feed the silkworms. Silkworms are actually the larva (caterpillars) of a kind of moth. Like most caterpillars, silkworms are fussy eaters and will only eat certain kinds of plant before they spin cocoons.

CHINESE SILK PRODUCTION

Coins and Markets in China

THE EARLIEST CHINESE TRADERS bartered (exchanged) goods, but by 1600 B.C., people were finding it easier to use tokens such as shells for buying and selling. The first metal coins date back to about 750 B.C., and were shaped like knives and spades. It was Qin Shi Huangdi, the first emperor, who introduced round coins. These had holes in the middle, so that they could be threaded on a cord for safe-keeping. The world's first paper money appeared in China in about A.D. 900.

There were busy markets in every Chinese town, which sold fruit, vegetables, rice, flour, eggs, and poultry and also cloth, medicine, pots, and pans. In the Tang dynasty capital, Chang'an (Xian), trading was limited to two large areas—the West and East Markets. This was so that government officials could control prices and trading standards.

CHINESE TRADING
Goods from China changed hands many times on the Silk Road to Europe. Trade moved in both directions. Porcelain, tea, and silk were carried westward. Silver, gold, and precious stones were transported back into China from central and southern Asia.

raw silk　　*Chinese tea*

CASH CROPS
Tea is trampled into chests in this European view of tea production in China. The work looks hard and the conditions cramped. For years, China had traded with India and Arabia. In the 1500s, it began a continuous trading relationship with Europe. By the early 1800s, China supplied 90 percent of all the world's tea.

MAKE A PELLET DRUM
You will need: large roll of masking tape, pencil, thin cream card, thick card, scissors, glue and brush, 1 in. x 12 in. thin gray card, thread, ruler, needle, bamboo stick, paint (red, green, and black), water pot, paintbrush, 2 colored beads.

1 Use the outside of the tape roll to draw 2 circles on thin cream card. Use the inside to draw 2 smaller circles on thick card. Cut out, as shown.

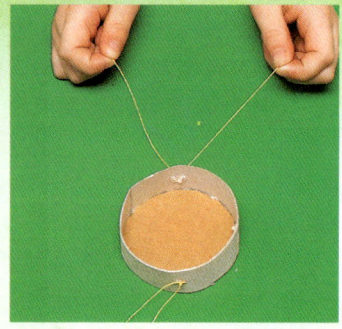

2 Glue gray strip around one of smaller circles. Make 2 small holes each side of strip. Cut 2 pieces of thread, 8 inches long. Pass through the holes and tie a knot.

3 Use the scissors to make a hole in the side of the strip for the bamboo stick. Push the stick through, as shown. Tape the stick to the hole.

THE SILK ROAD
The trading route known as the Silk Road developed during the Han dynasty. The road ran for almost 7,000 miles, from Chang'an (modern Xian), through Yumen and Kasghar, to Persia and the shores of the Mediterranean Sea. Merchants carried tea, silk, and other goods from one trading post to the next.

FROM DISTANT LANDS
A foreign trader rides on his camel during the Tang dynasty. At this time, China's international trade began to grow rapidly. Most trade was still handled by foreign merchants, among them Armenians, Jews, and Persians. They traded their wares along the Silk Road, bringing goods to the court at the Tang dynasty capital, Chang'an.

BUYERS AND SELLERS
This picture shows a typical Chinese market in about 1100. It appears on a Song dynasty scroll, and is thought to show the market in the capital, Kaifeng, at the time of the New Year festival.

Twist the drum handle to make the little balls rattle. In the hubbub of a street market, a merchant could shake a pellet drum to gain the attention of passers by. He would literally drum up trade!

4 Tape the stick handle down securely at the top of the drum. Take the second small circle and glue it firmly into place. This seals the drum.

5 Draw matching designs of your choice on the 2 thin cream card circles. Cut out a decorative edge. Paint the designs and allow them to dry.

6 Paint the bamboo stick handle red and allow to dry. When the stick is dry, glue the 2 decorated circles into position on top of the 2 smaller circles.

7 Thread the 2 beads. Make sure the thread is long enough to allow the beads to hit the center of the drum. Tie as shown. Cut off any excess.

COINS AND MARKETS IN CHINA

Money and Trade in India

TRADE WITH DISTANT COUNTRIES has been important for India as far back as the ancient civilization of the Indus Valley. Later, trade routes became established up and down the length of India, and also to faraway places. Luxurious and precious goods, such as spices, jewels, ebony, ivory, and teak, were the main trade objects. One highly prized import was silk from China.

The first coins in India—which had very simple designs—date from about 500 B.C. They were probably introduced from Persia (modern Iran). By about 100 B.C., coins were widely used to pay for goods and services in city markets and courts, but were less common in villages, where people simply exchanged goods, or bartered. Bartering remained the normal way of trading for villagers until Mughal times (from 1526 onward).

Many different types of coins were produced, including square ones. Some had portraits of kings and gods on them, and were often inscribed with the name of the ruling king. They were made of gold, silver, copper, and alloys (mixes of metals). Silver seems to have been used frequently for the best coins, but this material sometimes ran short when it was in demand for making statues and ornaments.

HEADS OR TAILS
A king of the Gupta dynasty with a stringed instrument is shown on a gold coin dating from around A.D. 350. Portraits of ancient Hindu royalty were most often to be found on coins. Few other likenesses, such as sculptures or carvings, exist of ancient Hindu kings.

SHELLING OUT
Cowrie shells were used as currency (money) in coastal areas. They were also used inland, when precious metals were scarce. Cowries were the lowest form of coinage. In one court poem, it is said that King Ramapala of Bengal paid his army in cowrie shells.

TRADE ROAD FOR SILK
The Silk Road stretched for more than 7,000 miles, from China to Anatolia (modern Turkey) and beyond. It was a trade route for items such as silk, jewels, and spices. Travelers along the Silk Road also brought new ideas. China and Central Asia were introduced to Buddhism, and many Chinese pilgrims came to India via the Silk Road.

32 INDIA 6000 B.C.–A.D. 1750

TRADING IN SPICE
Saffron is an aromatic spice grown in northern India. Sandalwood is a musky-smelling wood, produced mainly in the south. Both were rare and valuable, and were among India's most prized trading items. They were exported to the Middle East and to China.

ARAB TRADING VESSEL
This painting shows an Arab trading ship. The Indian Ocean became an important trading zone after the rise of Islam in the A.D. 600s. The ocean linked the powerful empires of Arabia to eastern lands, including India, Southeast Asia, and China. Muslim merchants ruled the seas from the A.D. 700s, until the coming of the Europeans in the 1500s.

TRADERS TRAVELING TOGETHER
A wall mural from Rajasthan shows a caravan (a group of merchants traveling together). Camels were ideal for travel in western Rajasthan, which is mostly desert. From Mughal times, Rajasthani merchants were famous throughout India for being good at making money.

COIN MEDALLION
A gold coin of the Mughal emperor Jahangir (1605-1627) has a portrait on one side and a Persian inscription on the other. This coin was probably not used in trade, but was instead worn as a sign of the emperor's favor. Using coins as decorations—especially if the coins were made of gold—dates back to the A.D. 100s. At that time, Roman coins were made into jewelry in the southern regions of India.

MONEY AND TRADE IN INDIA

Textiles Industry in India

MAKING TEXTILES HAS ALWAYS BEEN an important activity in India. There are records of ancient Romans buying Indian cloth, so the textile trade must have been well established by then. Since fabric does not last well, there are few examples from before A.D. 900, but sculptures show the kinds of cotton cloth that were made. In Buddhist and Hindu sculptures, clothing is usually light and draws attention to the shape of the body.

India's textiles show a lot of different influences. Silk originally came from China, but from about A.D. 100, it was produced in India and became an important export. From about 1100, Turkish and then Persian invaders introduced floral designs. Fine carpets also began to be made following Persian traditions and styles. Some places began to specialize in the production or sale of textiles. In Mughal times (from 1526), silks and muslin (fine cotton cloth) were produced at Ahmedabad, Surat and Dhaka, and Kanchipuram, near Madras, became known for its fine silk saris. The Coromandel coast, Gujarat and Bengal all became textile export centers.

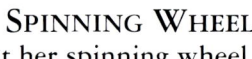

DRAPED GARMENT
A red sandstone figure from Jamalpur dates from about A.D. 400, and shows the Buddha dressed in a fine muslin garment. Many clothes in ancient India were draped and folded rather than sewn.

SPINNING WHEEL
A woman sits at her spinning wheel. Weavers were important, because Indian fabrics were in great demand in Europe.

MAKE A PRINTING BLOCK

You will need: paper, felt-tipped pen, scissors, halved raw potato, blunt knife, 8 in. x 6 in. piece of beige calico fabric, iron, scrap paper, paints, paintbrush.

1 Copy the pattern shown here on a sheet of paper. You can invent your own Indian design, if you prefer. Carefully cut out the pattern.

2 Place the cut-out pattern on the cut surface of the halved potato. Draw around the outline of the pattern with a felt-tipped pen.

3 Use the knife to cut the potato around the pattern. Your pattern should be raised about ¼ inch above the rest of the potato half.

PERSIAN-STYLE CARPET
This fine, wool carpet is decorated with floral patterns. In Mughal times, many fine carpets like this one were produced in India. Carpet weaving was a skill learned in the northwest of India from Persian craftspeople.

indigo block   madder

RED AND BLUE DYES
Dark-red dye made from the root of the madder plant, and violet-blue dye made from the leaves of the indigo plant, were used to dye textiles during Mughal times. Little is known about the way in which textiles were dyed in earlier times.

PRINTING COTTON CLOTH
A Punjabi man prints a pattern on a piece of cotton with a printing block. Dyes for cotton cloth were usually made from vegetables.

HUNTING COAT
This satin hunting coat has scenes and animals of the hunt embroidered on it in silk. It is typical of the type of dress worn by Mughal nobles.

Printing blocks were used in Mughal times to decorate fabric for festivals and other special occasions.

4 Ask an adult to help you iron the fabric. Lay the ironed fabric on top of scrap paper. Apply paint to part of your printing block with a paintbrush.

5 Brush a different color of paint on your printing block. Give the block an even coat of paint that is not too heavy. Do not drench the block.

6 Press the printing block on the fabric a few times. When the paint design starts to fade, apply more paint to the block with the paintbrush.

7 When the print design has dried, add some colorful details. Try out different colors on your printing block, or change the pattern on the fabric.

TEXTILES INDUSTRY IN INDIA

Japanese Peasant Farmers

Until the 1900s, most Japanese people lived in the countryside and made their living either by fishing, or by farming small plots of land. Japanese farmers grew crops for various reasons. They grew rice to sell to the samurai warriors and to pay taxes. Barley, millet, wheat, and vegetables were used for their own food. Traditionally, Japanese society was divided into four main classes—samurai, peasant farmers, craftspeople, and merchants. Samurai were the most highly respected. Farmers and craftspeople came next, because they produced useful goods. Merchants were ranked the lowest, because they produced nothing themselves.

During the Tokugawa period (1600–1868) in Japan, towns and cities grew bigger, small industries developed, and trade increased. Farmers began to sell their crops to people who had no land of their own. For the first time, some farmers had money to spend on better clothes, houses, and more food.

WRESTLERS
Sumo wrestling has long been a favorite sport in Japan. It developed from religious rituals and from games held at farmers' festivals in the countryside. Sumo wrestlers are usually very fat. They use their massive weight to overbalance their opponents.

TERRACING
It was difficult to find enough flat land for growing crops in Japan, so terraces were cut, like steps, into the steep hillsides. Farmland could be shaken by earthquakes or ruined by floods. In years when the harvests failed, there was often a famine.

RICE FARMING
Planting out tiny rice seedlings in shallow, muddy water was tiring, back-breaking work. Rice farming was introduced to Japan soon after 300 B.C. Most varieties of rice need to grow in flooded fields, called tanbo (paddy-fields). To provide extra food, farmers also reared fish in the tanbo.

FAVOURITE FOODS
Soybeans and daikon (white radishes) were two popular Japanese foods. The Japanese developed storage methods that would allow them to last for months. The radishes were covered in earth, and the beans were dried to provide essential winter food supplies. Farmers grew vegetables like these in small garden plots or in terraced fields.

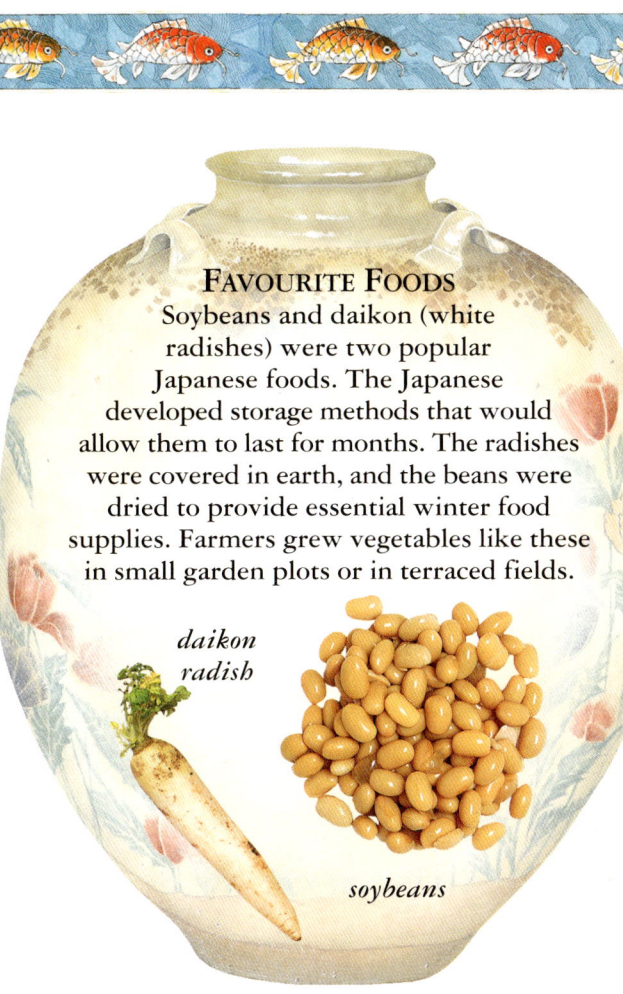

daikon radish

soybeans

A HARD LIFE
A woman farmworker carries heavy baskets of grain on a wooden yoke. Although farmers were respected, their lives were often very hard. Until the late 1800s, they had to pay heavy taxes to the emperor or the local lord, and were not free to leave their lord's land. They were also forbidden from wearing silk clothes, and drinking tea and sake (rice wine).

THRESHING
Japanese farmers are busy threshing wheat in this photograph taken in the late 1800s. Although this picture is relatively recent, the method of threshing has changed little over the centuries. The workers at the far right and the far left are separating the grains of wheat from the stalks, by pulling them through wooden sieves. In the background, one worker carries a huge bundle of wheat stalks, while another stands ready with a rake and a winnowing fan. The fan was used to remove the chaff from the grain by tossing the grain in the air, so that the wind blew the chaff away.

JAPANESE PEASANT FARMERS

Poor Soils and Hot Sun in Greece

Most ancient Greeks lived in the countryside and worked as farmers. The mountainous landscape, poor, stony soil, and hot, dry climate restricted what crops they grew and which animals they kept, but olive trees and bees flourished. Olives provided oil, and bees supplied honey (the main sweetener in the ancient Greek diet) and wax. Unlike ancient Egypt and China, grain, such as barley, was difficult to grow. The land used for grain production had to be left fallow every other year to recover its fertility. Country people kept oxen to pull plows and drag heavy loads, and they used donkeys to carry goods to the market. Rural areas also produced materials used by city craftspeople, such as timber, flax for linen, horn and bone for glue, and leather.

Country living was hazardous, because droughts, floods, wolves, and warfare threatened people's livelihoods. In time, another problem developed. As forests were cut down for timber and fuel, soil erosion increased, leaving even less fertile land. The search for new agricultural land prompted the growth of Greek colonies along the shores of the Mediterranean and the Black Sea.

Olive Harvest
This vase shows men shaking and beating the branches of an olive tree to bring down its fruit. Olives were eaten and also crushed to extract their oil. The oil was used for cooking, cleaning, as a medicine, and a fuel for lamps.

Food for the Pot
Meat was obtained through hunting and the rearing of domesticated animals. Hunting was considered a sport for the rich, but it was a serious business for the poor, who hoped to put extra food on their tables. Simple snares, nets, and slings were used to trap lizards and hares, and to bring down small birds.

Gone Fishing
Many Greeks lived near water. The sea, rivers, and lakes provided fish and shellfish, which were their main source of protein. Fish was smoked or salted for future use. Always at the mercy of storms and shipwreck, fishermen prayed to the sea god Poseidon to save them.

38   ANCIENT GREECE 2000 B.C.–146 B.C.

PLOWING WITH OXEN
This terra-cotta figure from Thebes shows a farmer plowing with two oxen. The plow was made of wood, but the part that broke up the earth was tipped with iron. Oxen were stronger and less expensive than horses, which made them ideal for heavy work. When oxen died, they yielded hides for leather in addition to horn, meat, sinew—which was used as twine, and fat that could be turned into candle tallow.

SNACKS
Drying food was a good way of preserving it in a warm country like Greece. The Greeks ate raisins and dried apricots as a dessert, or used them to sweeten other foods. Olives were another popular snack and appetizer.

olives
apricots
raisins

HARVEST GODDESS
Demeter was the goddess of grain and growth. She cared for plants, children, and young people. The first part of her name "deme" is an ancient word for the Earth, the second part, "meter," means mother. Farmers believed that their success depended on uncontrollable forces such as the rain, the Sun, and diseases that attacked plants and livestock. Special prayers and sacrifices were made to Demeter to ask for her help in preventing such disasters. Festivals were held in honor of the goddess at crucial times during the harvest, before plowing, when the grain began to sprout, and after it had been harvested.

POOR SOILS AND HOT SUN IN GREECE

Seafaring Greeks

THE MOUNTAINOUS LANDSCAPE of ancient Greece was too rocky for carts or chariots, so most people rode donkeys or walked. Sea travel was simpler—the many islands of the eastern Mediterranean made it possible to sail from one port to another without losing sight of land. Merchant ships were sailed, because they were too heavy to be rowed. Greek sailors had no compasses. By day, they relied on coastal landmarks, and at night, they navigated by the stars. However, neither method was reliable. A sudden storm could throw a ship off course or cause it to sink. Merchant ships carried olive oil, wool, wine, silver, fine pottery, and slaves. These goods were traded in return for wheat and timber, both of which were scarce in Greece. Other imported products included tin, copper, ivory, gold, silk, and cotton.

COINS
The gold coin above shows Zeus, ruler of the gods, throwing a thunderbolt. Coins were invented in Lydia (in present-day Turkey) around 635 B.C., and introduced to Greece soon afterward. Before that, the Greeks had used bars of silver and rods of iron as money. Greek coins were also made of silver, bronze, and electrum—a mixture of gold and silver.

SEA GOD
Poseidon was the god of the sea, horses, and earthquakes. Sailors prayed and made sacrifices to him, hoping for protection against storms, fogs, and pirates. He is usually pictured holding a trident, the three-pronged spear used by Greek fishermen. At the trading port of Corinth, the Isthmian Games were held every other year in honor of Poseidon.

HARD CURRENCY
The first coins may have been used to pay mercenary soldiers, rather than for trading and collecting taxes. The earliest coins usually bore a religious symbol or the emblem of a city. Only later did they show the head of a ruler. The coin on the right shows the sea god Poseidon with his trident. The coin on the left bears the rose of Rhodes. Many countries that traded with the Greeks copied their idea of using coins for money.

SHIPPING

The ship on the right is a sail-powered merchant ship. The crisscross lines represent a wooden and rope catwalk, which was stretched over the cargo and stored in an uncovered hold. Liquids such as wine and olive oil were transported and sold in long narrow pottery jars called amphorae, which could be neatly stacked in the hold. Merchant ships faced many dangers that could cause the loss of their cargo. Pirates and storms were the worst of these.

WEIGHING

Most dry goods were sold loose and had to be weighed on a scale such as this one. Officials would oversee the proceedings to make sure that they were fair. They stopped merchants and traders from cheating one another. In Athens, these officials were known as metronomoi. It was essential for merchants to familiarize themselves with the various systems of weights and measures used in different countries.

MARKET STALLS

The agora, or market place, was to be found in the center of every Greek town. Market stalls sold a wide variety of goods including meat, vegetables, eggs, cheese, and fish. Fish was laid out on marble slabs to keep it cool and fresh.

clams *shrimps* *mussels*

RIDING

Mountainous countryside made traveling overland difficult in Greece. The few roads that did exist were in poor condition. For most people, walking was the only way to reach a destination. Horses were usually only used by wealthy people to travel on. Donkeys and mules were used by tradesmen to transport large loads. Longer journeys were made by boat.

SEAFARING GREEKS

Ancient Greek Workshops

THE ARTISTS AND CRAFTSPEOPLE of ancient Greece were admired for the quality of their work. They produced many objects of art including beautiful pottery, fine jewelry, and impressive sculptures. Materials they worked with included stone, gold, silver, glass, gem stones, and bronze. They also used wood, leather, bone, ivory, and horn. Most goods were made on a small scale in workshops that surrounded the market place. A craftsman might work on his own, or with the help of his family and a slave or two. In the larger workshops of such cities as Athens, slaves labored to produce bulk orders of popular goods. These might include shields, pottery, and metalwork, which were traded around the Mediterranean Sea for a large profit.

BULK PRODUCTION
Above is a terra-cotta mold, and on the right, the casting taken from it. Making a mold was a skilled and time-consuming task. Using a mold made it possible to produce items faster and more cheaply than carving each piece individually.

RAW MATERIALS
Gold was an expensive import and was usually used to make luxury items such as jewelry. Less commonly, it was used to decorate statues and to make gold coins. Clay was used in the production of a wide variety of crafts, from vases to statuettes.

gold *clay*

PANATHENAIC VASE
You will need: balloon, bowl, white glue, water, newspaper, two rolls of masking tape, black pen, scissors, sheet of paper 17 in. x 12 in., card, pencil, paintbrush, black and cream paint.

1 Blow up the balloon. Cover it with two layers of papier mâché (paper soaked in one part glue, two parts water). Set on one side to dry.

2 Using a roll of masking tape as a guide, draw and cut out two holes at the top and bottom of the balloon. Throw away the popped balloon.

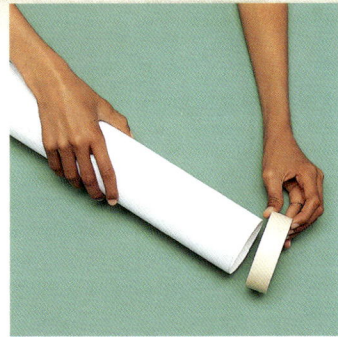

3 Roll the sheet of paper into a tube. Make sure that it will fit through the middle of the roll of masking tape. Secure the tube with tape or glue.

Vase Painting
This black-figure vase painting originated in Corinth around 700 B.C. The black-figure style was succeeded by a red-figure style, invented in Athens around 525 B.C. The painters were not all anonymous artisans. Many were widely recognized as artists in their own right, who signed their works. The export of vases like this became a major source of income for both cities.

Hot Work
In this scene, two blacksmiths are forging metal at a brick furnace. Metal goods were expensive to produce. The furnaces themselves were fueled by charcoal (burnt wood), which was expensive to make because wood was scarce in Greece. In addition, supplies of metal often had to be imported, sometimes from great distances. For example, tin—which was mixed with local copper to make bronze—was brought from southern Spain.

Amphorae like this one were given as prizes at the Panathenaic games. They were decorated with sports images.

Gold Pectoral
This gold pectoral, made on the island of Rhodes in the seventh century B.C., was worn across the breast. Gold was rare in Greece. It was usually imported at great expense from surrounding areas, such as Egypt and Asia Minor.

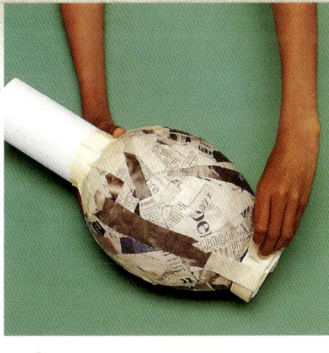

4 Pull the tube through the middle of the balloon. Tape into place. Pull a roll of masking tape over the bottom of the paper tube and tape.

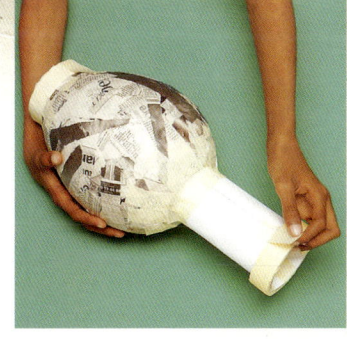

5 Tape the second roll of masking tape to the top of the tube. Make sure that both rolls are securely attached at both ends of the paper tube.

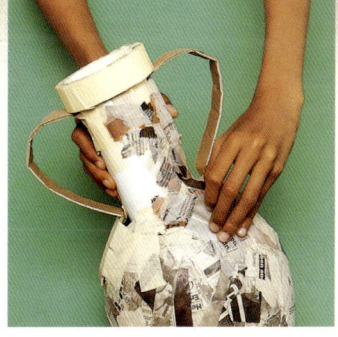

6 Cut two strips of card, 6 in. long. Attach them to either side of the vase, as seen above. Cover the entire vase with papier mâché, and allow to dry.

7 Using a pencil, copy the pattern shown on the vase in the picture above on your vase. Carefully paint the pattern, and set on one side to dry.

ANCIENT GREEK WORKSHOPS

Shopping Roman Style

In most large towns in the Roman Empire, shops spread out from the forum and along the main streets. Shops were usually small, family-run businesses. At the start of day, shutters or blinds would be taken from the shop front and goods put on display. Noise would soon fill the air, as bakers, butchers, fishmongers, and fruit and vegetable sellers all began crying out that their produce was the best and cheapest. Joints of meat might be hung from a pole, and precooked food, grains, and oils would be sold from pots set into a stone counter. Other shops sold pottery lamps and bronze lanterns, kitchen pots and pans, and knives, and some traders repaired shoes or laundered cloth. Hammering and banging coming from the workshops at the back added to the clamor of a busy main street.

Roman Money
The same currency was used throughout the Roman Empire. Coins were made of gold, silver, and bronze. Shoppers kept their money in purses made of cloth or leather, and in wooden boxes.

How's Business?
This carving shows merchants discussing prices and profits, while an assistant brings out goods from the stockroom. Most Roman shops were single rooms, with storerooms and workshops at the back.

Going to Market
This is a view of Trajan's Market, which was a five-story group of shops set into a hillside in Rome. Most Roman towns had covered halls or central markets like this, where shops were rented out to traders.

A Roman Delicatessen
About 1,700 years ago, this was the place to buy good food in Ostia, the seaport closest to Rome. Bars, inns, and cafés were fitted with stone counters that were often decorated with colored marble. At lunchtime, bars like this would be busy with customers enjoying a meal.

A Butcher's Shop
A Roman butcher uses a cleaver to prepare chops, while a customer waits for her order. Butchers' shops have changed very little over the ages—pork, lamb, and beef were sold, and sausages were popular, too. On the right hangs a steelyard, a metal bar with a pan-like scale, for weighing meat.

Dishing it Up
These are the remains of a shop that sold food. Set into the marble counter are big pottery containers, called dolia. These were used for displaying and serving food, such as beans and lentils. They were also used for keeping jars of wine cool on hot summer days. The containers could be covered with wooden or stone lids, to keep out the flies.

SHOPPING ROMAN STYLE

Celtic Farmers of Europe

THE CELTS WERE FARMING PEOPLE who lived in central and northern Europe—they cleared fields, planted crops, and bred livestock. They also fenced meadowland, and kept out their grazing animals until they had cut and dried the meadow grass to make hay for winter fodder. Farmers used an iron-tipped plow, pulled by oxen, to turn over the soil in their fields and prepare the ground for planting. Seeds of grain were scattered by hand on plowed land in early springtime. The crops were ready to harvest in late summer and fall. The Celts' most important crops were wheat, oats, and barley, which were cooked to make porridge, or ground into flour.

The most common farm animals were pigs, cattle, sheep, and goats. In addition to producing meat, animals provided milk (used to make butter and cheese), wool (spun and woven into cloth), and hides (which were tanned to make leather). The Celts also reared ducks and geese, for meat and eggs. Manure from animals and birds was used as a fertilizer on the fields. In some areas, Celtic farmers dug pits for marl (natural lime) to spread on their land as fertilizer.

BULL'S EYE
Cattle were the most important farm animals in many Celtic lands. Oxen were used to pull carts and farm machinery, as well as for food. All cattle were highly prized, and were the main source of wealth for many farmers. Irish myths and legends tell of daring raids, when Celtic warriors galloped off to attack enemy farms and take all their cattle away.

SICKLE AND HOE
As crops grew in the fields, the Celtic farmer used a hoe (*right*) to keep the weeds down. The crops were harvested with a sharp, curved sickle (*above*). This hoe and sickle date from the La Tène era (450–50 B.C.). Farming tools such as these were made by blacksmiths out of iron. Grain crops and hay were sometimes cut by an animal-drawn reaping machine, called a vallus. It was made of wood, with iron cutting blades.

WILD PAIR
The Celts raised pigs on their farms as well as hunting wild boar in the woods. Farm pigs were much smaller and thinner than European pigs today. They had long legs and stripy, bristly hair. In Celtic art, the boar was a symbol of great strength and power. These two little bronze pigs were probably made as offerings to the gods.

46 THE CELTS 800 B.C.–A.D. 1066

RARE BREED
The Soay sheep is an ancient breed that is rare today. It is similar to the sheep kept by Celtic farmers. It is small, nimble, and hardy, and has long horns. Soay sheep do not need shearing—their fleece sheds naturally in the summer. The wool can then be combed or pulled out by hand.

GRACEFUL GOOSE
This stone slab was carved in Scotland, in about A.D. 450. It shows a goose turning around to preen its tail feathers. Geese were kept for their meat, eggs, and grease. Goose grease could be rubbed on sore, dry skin, and it was also used to soften and waterproof leather. Although the evidence has not survived, it seems likely that soft goose feathers were used to make warm bedding, too.

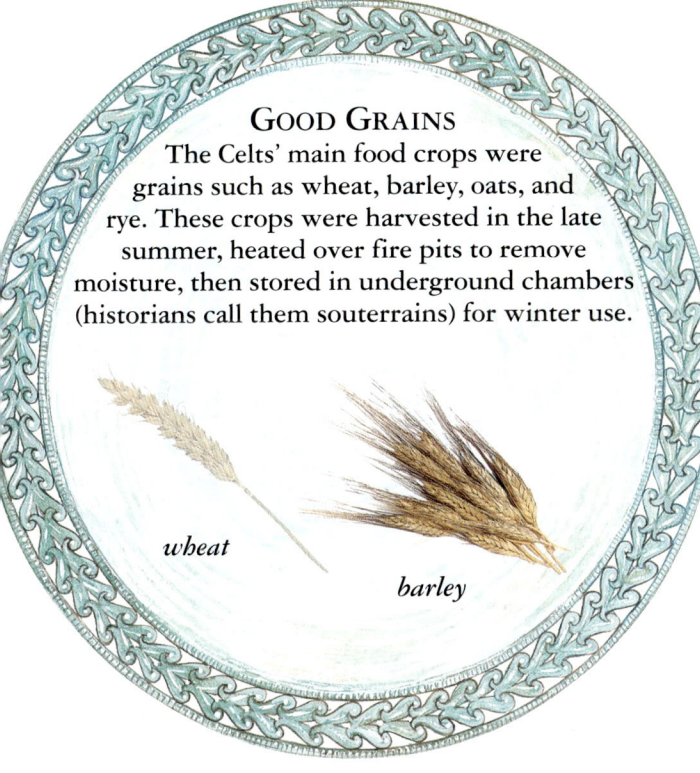

GOOD GRAINS
The Celts' main food crops were grains such as wheat, barley, oats, and rye. These crops were harvested in the late summer, heated over fire pits to remove moisture, then stored in underground chambers (historians call them souterrains) for winter use.

wheat

barley

RIDGE AND FURROW
Ancient ridges and furrows in southwest England (*above*) were created by late medieval farmers using techniques that may have been developed by the Celts. During the Celtic era, farmers began to move away from the light, well-drained soils on hilltops and slopes, to clear new fields on the heavier, wetter, but more fertile land at the bottom of valleys. They invented heavy plows, fitted with wheels and pulled by oxen, to help cultivate this land.

Celtic Trade Routes

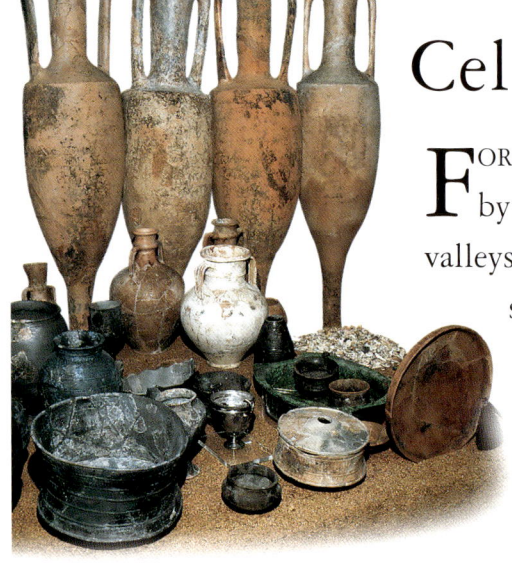

For thousands of years, different parts of Europe have been linked by long-distance trade. Well-known routes followed great river valleys, such as the Rhine, the Rhône, and the Danube, or connected small ports along the coasts, from Ireland to Portugal. As early as 600 B.C., eastern traders from the Mediterranean claimed to have sailed through the Straits of Gibraltar and over the sea to the British Isles. After around 200 B.C., the Celts began to build fortified settlements as centers of government, crafts, and trade. Some grew up around existing hill forts or villages, others occupied fresh sites. The Romans called them "oppida," the Latin word for towns. Some of the oppida were very large; Manching, in southern Germany, covered about 940 acres, and its protective walls were 4½ miles long.

Wine Lovers
The Celts were very fond of wine, which they imported from Italy. Roman wine merchants transported their wine in tall pottery jars called amphorae. You can see four amphorae at the back of this picture.

High Value
Celts learned how to make coins from the Macedonians, who lived in eastern Europe. The first Celtic coins were made of pure precious metals, such as gold and silver. They were made by stamping a metal disc between two dies (molds).

Small Change
During the Celtic era in Europe, coins were made from alloys (mixed metals) that contained only a small amount of silver or gold. These coins were much less valuable than the earlier, pure metal ones. This alloy coin was made around 100 B.C. in western France.

Make a Wagon
You will need: white card, ruler, felt-tip pen, scissors, balsa wood, white glue, masking tape, sandpaper, compass, paint and paintbrush, drawing pins, bradawl, leather thong.

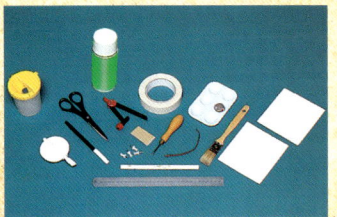

1 Take a piece of stiff white card measuring 11½ x 6¼ in. Using a ruler and felt-tip pen, draw lines ¾ in. in from the edges of the card.

2 Make cuts in the corners of the card, as shown. Score along the lines and fold the edges up to make a box shape. This is the body of the wagon.

3 Take a piece of card 10½ x 4½ in. Take two pieces of balsa wood 8 in. long. Stick them across the card, 1½ in. in from the two ends.

KEY
- Iron
- Tin
- Amphorae (wine jars)
- Amber
- Salt

LONG-DISTANCE TRADE
Celtic merchants and craftspeople in different lands were linked together by a network of trade routes, leading north-south and east-west. Few traders would have traveled the whole distance of any one route. Instead, merchants from different countries met in trading towns. Valuable goods might be bought and sold several times along a trade route before reaching their final owner.

TOWN WALLS
Oppida were surrounded by strong, defensive walls. These ruined ones are from a Celtic town in southern France. Within the walls, houses, streets, and crafts workshops were laid out in well-planned, orderly rows.

This model wagon is based on the remains of funeral wagons found buried in Celtic graves. The Celts used wagons that were more roughly made, but easier to steer for carrying heavy loads.

4 Take two sticks of balsa wood 10¼ in. and 4¼ in. long. Sand the end of the long stick to make an indent to fit against the short piece. Glue together.

5 Use the compass to draw four circles, each 4 in. in diameter, out of card. Next, carefully cut out the circles, as shown above.

6 Glue the box to the piece of card. Attach the wheels to the balsa wood shafts by pressing a drawing pin through the center of each wheel.

7 Make two holes in the front of the wagon with a bradawl. Thread the leather thong through the holes, and attach the steering pole. Paint the wagon silver.

CELTIC TRADING ROUTES

Long-Distance Trade in Viking Times

COINS
These silver coins were found on the site of the market place in Birka. They were minted in Hedeby in around 800.

THE VIKINGS were very successful merchants. Their home trade was based in northern European towns such as Hedeby in Denmark, Birka in Sweden, and Kaupang in Norway. As they settled new lands, their trade routes began to spread far and wide. They traded in countries as far apart as Britain, Iceland, and Greenland.

In about 860, Swedish Vikings opened up new routes eastward through the lands of the Slavs. They rowed and sailed down rivers such as the Volga, Volkhov, and Dniepr. Viking sailors hauled their boats around rapids, and fought off attacks from local peoples. Their trade turned the cities of Holmgard (Novgorod) and Könugard (Kiev) into powerful states. This marked the birth of Russia as a nation. Merchants crossed the Black Sea and the Caspian Sea. They traveled on to Constantinople (Istanbul), the capital of the Byzantine empire, and to the great Arab city of Baghdad.

Viking warehouses were crammed with casks of wine from Germany and bales of woolen cloth from England. There were furs and walrus ivory from the Arctic, and timber and iron from Scandinavia. Vikings also traded in wheat from the British Isles and rye from Russia.

MAKING MONEY
This disk is a die—a metal stamp used to punch the design on the face of a coin. The die is from York, in England. It has a sword design.

AMBER KING
This carved amber king is a piece from a board game. Amber was exported from the lands around the Baltic Sea. It was much prized by traders and by craftspeople, who also made it into jewelry and lucky charms.

MAKE A COIN AND DIE

You will need: self-drying clay and tool, board, rolling pin, scissors, compass, pencil, paper, white glue, brush, paintbrush, bronze and silver paint.

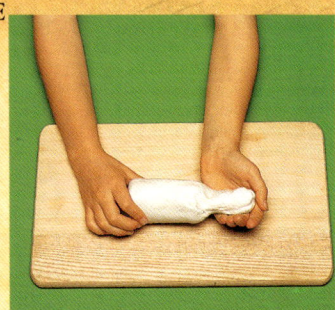

1 Roll out a large cylinder of clay and model a short, thick handle at one end. This is the die. Leave it in a warm place to harden and dry.

2 Cut out a circle from paper. It should be about the same size as the end of the die. Draw a simple shape on the paper circle, with a pencil.

3 Cut the paper circle in half. Cut out the shape as shown. If you find it hard to cut the shape out, you could ask an adult to cut it out with a craft knife.

EASTERN CONNECTIONS
Trade networks in the East linked with older routes, such as the Silk Road to China. Silk, jewelry, and spices were brought by camel from the Far East. In Baghdad's markets, Vikings bought these things in return for furs, beeswax, and slaves.

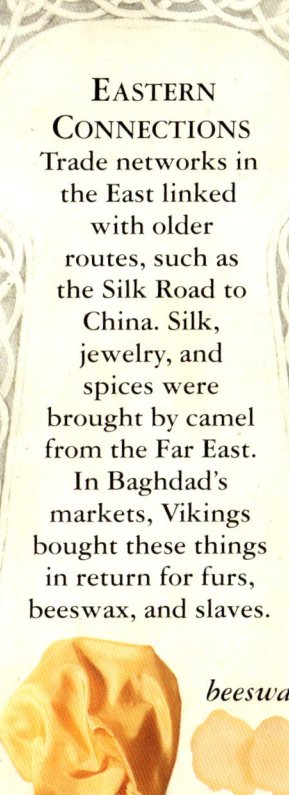

beeswax

silk

TRADE MAP
The routes taken by Viking traders fanned out south and east from their homelands. In addition to exotic goods from the East, everyday items such as salt, pottery, and wool were brought back from western Europe.

scales

weights

FAIR TRADING
Scales and weights were used by Viking merchants wherever they traded. Some could be folded up inside a small case.

scales

The first coins to show Viking kings were minted in England.

4 Glue the cut paper pieces to the end of the die with white glue. You may need to trim the pieces if they are too big to fit on the end.

5 Viking dies would have been made from bronze, or some other metal. Paint your die a bronze color. Make sure you paint an even coat.

6 Roll some more clay. Use the die to stamp an impression into the clay. This is your first coin. You can make as many as you like.

7 Use a modeling tool to cut around the edge of the coin. Make more coins from the left-over clay. Allow the coins to dry and harden, then paint them.

LONG-DISTANCE TRADE IN VIKING TIMES

North American Trading

NATIVE AMERICAN PEOPLES have a long tradition of trading. The Hopewell civilizations of about A.D. 200 brought metals and other materials to their centers around the Ohio valley. The Calusas in southern Florida had a vast trade network, both inland and across the sea to the Bahamas and Cuba. Many people would travel long distances to buy and sell goods at a regular meeting place. Although some tribes, or nations, used wampum (shell money), most swapped their goods. People from settled villages exchanged agricultural products, such as corn and tobacco for buffalo hides, baskets, and eagle feathers from nomadic tribes. When European traders arrived, in the 1600s, they exchanged furs and hides for horses, guns, cotton cloth, and metal tools. Early trading posts, such as the Hudson's Bay Company, were built by Europeans. These posts were usually on rivers that could be reached easily by canoe.

BASKETS FOR GOODS
Crafts, such as this Salish basket, were sometimes traded (or swapped) between tribes, and later with Europeans. Native Americans wanted woolen blankets, and European traders eagerly sought bison robes.

WAMPUM SNAPSHOT
A Mohawk chief, King Hendrick of the League of Five Nations, was painted on a visit to Queen Anne's court in London in 1710. He holds a wampum belt made from shells. These were made to record historic events, such as the formation of the League of Five Nations of the Iroquois.

COLONIAL TRADERS
A native hunter in Canada offers beaver skins to colonial fur traders in 1777. They would probably have been made into beaver hats. Beaver fur was the most important item the Woodlands nations had to trade, since competition between Europeans for animal skins was fierce. This trade was partly to blame for many tribal conflicts. The Iroquois were renowned beaver hunters who ruthlessly guarded their hunting territory.

52 NORTH AMERICAN INDIANS 10,000 B.C.–A.D. 1924

SHELL SHOW
A Plains man holds up a wampum belt decorated with shells. The belts were usually associated with the Iroquois and Algonquians, who used them as currency, for trade, and to record tribal history. Quahog clam shells were strung together to make a long belt with patterns that described tribal agreements and treaties. Even colonists used them as currency when there were no coins around.

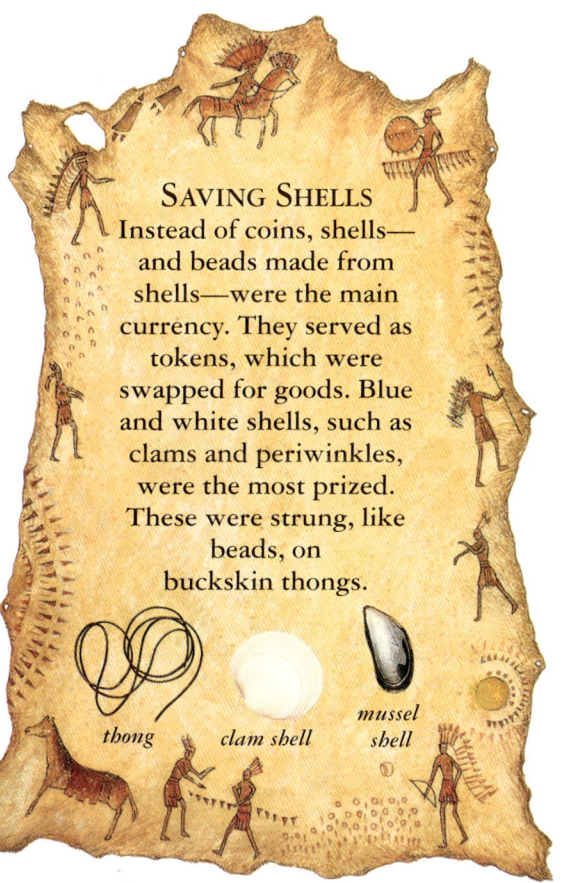

SAVING SHELLS
Instead of coins, shells—and beads made from shells—were the main currency. They served as tokens, which were swapped for goods. Blue and white shells, such as clams and periwinkles, were the most prized. These were strung, like beads, on buckskin thongs.

thong   clam shell   mussel shell

TRADING POSTS
Native Americans would gather in the Hudson's Bay trading post. In return for bringing pelts (animal furs), they would be given European goods. Many would be useful, such as iron tools, utensils, and colored cloth. Firearms and liquor traded from around 1650 did the tribes more harm than good. As trade increased, more trappers and hunters used the trading posts. Later, some of the fur trading posts became military forts, and they attracted settlers, who then built towns around them.

NORTH AMERICAN TRADING   53

Arctic Trapping and Trade

BEFORE 1600, few Europeans had visited the Arctic, but those that did returned with tales of waters teeming with whales and other sea creatures. European whaling ships were soon arriving in larger numbers to slaughter whales.

The whaling industry boomed during the 1700s, and became important to the livelihoods of the arctic peoples. By 1800, however, the Europeans had slaughtered so many whales that they faced extinction. As the whaling industry began to decline, European merchants soon realized that the soft fur of arctic mammals, such as sea otters and foxes, would fetch a high price in Europe. They traded with local hunters for these skins, setting up trading posts across the Arctic. In every region, the fur trade was controlled by the nation that had explored there first. Russia controlled all trade in Alaska, and Britain controlled business in Canada.

Arctic peoples came to rely on European trade for metal tools and weapons. Many abandoned their traditional life of hunting. Instead, they trapped mammals for their skins and sold them to the merchants. Arctic peoples entered troubled times. Diseases previously unknown in the region, such as measles and tuberculosis, killed thousands of people.

SKINS FOR SALE
The skins of seals and arctic foxes hang in a store in northwestern Greenland. During the 1800s and early 1900s, otter, fox, and mink fur became extremely popular in Europe. European merchants made huge profits from the trade, but paid arctic hunters low rates for trapping these valuable animals.

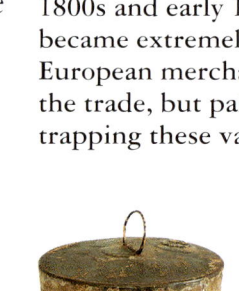

CONVENIENCE FOOD
In 1823, this tin of veal was prepared for Sir William Parry's expedition to the Arctic. European explorers, whalers, and traders introduced many foods to the native arctic peoples. Local trappers exchanged furs for food and other goods. However, some arctic people began to rely on the food provided by the traders, rather than hunting for their own food.

TRADING POST
This engraving, from around 1900, shows an Inuit hunter loading his sled with European goods at a trading post in the far north of Canada. By the mid-1800s, fortified posts such as this had sprung up all over Arctic North America. The British Hudson Bay Trading Company, which was set up in the 1820s, became very wealthy after exploiting Canada's natural resources.

Addicted to Alcohol

Whisky was traded throughout the Arctic in the 1800s and 1900s. In addition to goods made from metal, merchants introduced European foods and stimulants, such as tea, coffee, sugar, alcohol, and tobacco, to the Arctic. Many arctic hunters became addicted to liquor, such as whisky. This made them rely even more heavily on traders who could supply them with alcohol.

Scrimshaw

During the long arctic nights or lengthy voyages across the ocean, European explorers, sailors, and traders occupied their time carving pictures and patterns on whale bones and walrus tusks. This work was called scrimshaw. First, a design was scratched in the bone or tusk, using a knife or needle. Then the artist made the picture visible by rubbing soot into the scratches.

soot

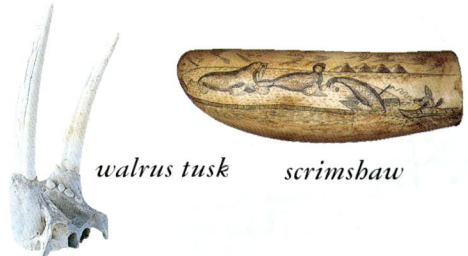
walrus tusk   *scrimshaw*

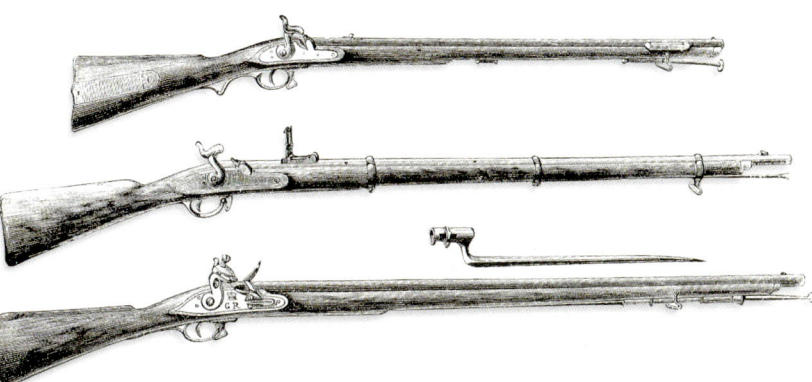

Powerful Weapon

This engraving shows a selection of British rifles from the 1840s. During the 1800s and 1900s, European guns and rifles transformed traditional hunting methods in the Arctic. Rifles were much more accurate than the old arctic weapons—bows and arrows—and could target prey from a much greater distance.

Goods for Trade

In this engraving, local hunters trade with Europeans in a local store. Hundreds of metal tools and weapons were traded by Europeans in the Arctic, most often for animal skins. European merchants also bartered rifles, saws, knives, drills, axes, and needles. The Inuit and other arctic groups soon came to depend on these valuable tools and weapons.

ARCTIC TRAPPING AND TRADE

Reclaiming Land in Mesoamerica

PEOPLE WHO LIVED IN DIFFERENT REGIONS of Mesoamerica (Central America) during Aztec and Mayan times used various methods to cultivate their land. Farmers in the rainforests grew corn (or maize), beans, and pumpkins in fields that they cleared by slashing and burning. They cut down thick, tangled bushes and vines, leaving the tallest trees standing. Then they burned all the chopped-down bushes and planted seeds in the ashes. Since the soil was only fertile for a few years, the fields were left to return to forest, and new ones were cleared. Mayan farmers also grew crops in raised fields. These were plots of land along the edges of rivers and streams, heaped with rich silt dug from the riverbed. Aztec farmers planted corn wherever they could, on steep rocky hillsides or the flat valley floor. They grew their biggest crops of fruit, flowers, and vegetables in gardens called chinampas. These were reclaimed from the marshy shallows along the shores of Lake Texcoco and around the island city of Tenochtitlan.

CORN GOD
This stone statue shows Yum Caax (Lord of the Forest Bushes), the Maya god of corn. It was found at Copan. All Mesoamerican people honored corn goddesses or gods, because the crop was so important.

DIGGING STICKS
Mesoamerican farmers had no tractors, horses, or heavy plows to help them prepare their fields. Instead, a sharp-bladed wooden digging stick, called an uictli, was used for planting seeds and hoeing weeds. Some farmers in Mesoamerica today find that digging sticks are more efficient than the kind of spade traditionally used in Europe.

FIELD WORK
In this painting by the Mexican artist Diego Rivera, Aztecs are shown using digging sticks to hoe fields of corn. You can see how dry the soil is. If the May rains failed, or frosts came early, a whole year's crop would be lost. Mesoamerican farmers made offerings to the rain god between March and October.

AZTEC & MAYA 2000 B.C.–A.D. 1600

Chinampa soil was made even more fertile by using human manure.

Sticky mud was collected from the lake bottom. Along with compost and manure, this mud was poured on top of the chinampas.

The chinampa was held together by stakes, thick water vegetation, and the tangled roots of trees.

FLOATING GARDENS
Chinampas were a type of floating garden. They were made by sinking layers of twigs and branches under the surface of the lake, and weighting them with stones. Chinampas were so productive that the government passed laws telling farmers when to sow seeds. This ensured a steady supply of vegetables and flowers for the markets.

SLASH AND BURN
Mesoamerican farmers used a technique called slash and burn to clear land for farming. Crops grew very quickly in Mesoamerica's warm climate.

VEGETARIANS
Many ordinary Mesoamerican people survived on a mainly vegetarian diet, based on corn and beans. This would be supplemented by other fresh fruits and vegetables in season. Meat and fish were expensive, luxury foods. Only rulers and nobles could afford to eat them every day.

FOREST FRUITS
This Aztec codex painting shows men and women gathering cocoa pods from trees. Cocoa was so valuable that it was sent as tribute to Tenochtitlan.

beans

prickly pear

RECLAIMING LAND IN MESOAMERICA

The Mesoamerican Market

THE MARKET PLACE was the heart of many Mesoamerican cities and towns. Traders, craftspeople, and farmers met there to exchange their produce. Many market traders were women. They sold cloth and cooking pots, made by themselves or their families, and corn, fruit, flowers, and vegetables grown by their husbands. In big cities, such as the trading center of Tlatelolco, government officials also sold exotic goods that had been sent to the Aztec rulers as a tribute (taxes) by conquered city-states. After the Aztecs conquered Tlatelolco in 1473, it soon became the largest market in Mesoamerica. It was reported that almost 50,000 people came there on the busiest days.

Long-distance trade was carried out by merchants called *pochteca*. Gangs of porters carried their goods. The work was often dangerous, but the rewards were great.

MERCHANT GOD
Yacatecuhtli was the Aztec god of merchants and traders. In the codex picture above, he is shown standing in front of a crossroads marked with footprints. Behind him (*right*), is a tired porter with a load of birds on his back.

CORN MARKET
Mesoamerican farmers grew many different varieties of corn, with cobs that were pale cream, bright yellow, and even deep blue. Their wives took the corn to market, since selling was women's work. This modern wall-painting shows Aztec women buying and selling corn in the great market at Tlatelolco. At the market, judges sat in raised booths, keeping a lookout for thieves and cheats.

MAKE A MAYAN POT
You will need: self-drying clay, board, rolling pin, masking tape, modeling tool, water bowl, small bowl, petroleum jelly, white glue, glue brush, yellow and black paint, paintbrush, water pot.

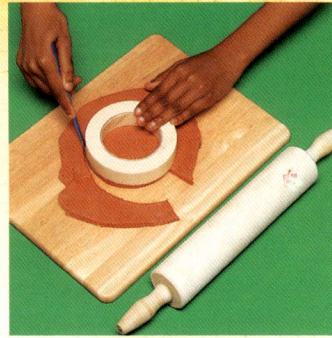

1 Roll out the clay until it is approximately ¼ in. thick. Cut out a base for the pot with a modeling tool. Use a roll of masking tape as a guide for size.

2 Roll out some long cylinders of clay. Coil them around the base of the pot to build up the sides. Join and smooth the clay with water as you go.

3 Model a lip at the top of the pot. Allow it to dry. Cover a small bowl with petroleum jelly. Make a lid by rolling out some clay. Place the clay over the bowl.

JOURNEY'S END
This modern painting shows merchants and porters arriving at the market city of Tlatelolco. Such travelers made long journeys to bring back valuable goods, such as shells, jade, and fig-bark paper. Young men who joined the merchants' guild were warned about tiredness, pain, and ambush on their travels.

BARTER
Mesoamerican people did not have coins. They bought and sold by bartering, exchanging the goods they wanted to sell for other peoples' goods of equal value. Costly items such as gold-dust, quetzal feathers, and cocoa beans were exchanged for goods they wanted to buy.

SKINS
Items such as puma, ocelot, and jaguar skins could fetch a high price at market.

colorful feathers   *cocoa beans*

MARKET PRODUCE
In Mexico today, many markets are still held on the same sites as ancient ones. Many of the same types of foodstuffs are on sale there. In this modern photograph, we see tomatoes, avocados, and vegetables that were also grown in Aztec times. Today, as in the past, most market traders and shoppers are women.

Mesoamerican potters made their pots by these coil or slab techniques. The potter's wheel was not used at all in Mesoamerica. The pots were sold at the local market.

4 Turn your pot upside-down and place it over the rolled-out clay. Trim the excess clay with a modeling tool by cutting around the top of the pot.

5 Use balls of clay to make a turtle to go on top of the lid. When both the lid and turtle are dry, use glue to stick the turtle to the center of the lid.

6 Roll three small balls of clay of exactly the same size for the pot's feet. When they are dry, glue them to the base of the pot. Make sure they are evenly spaced.

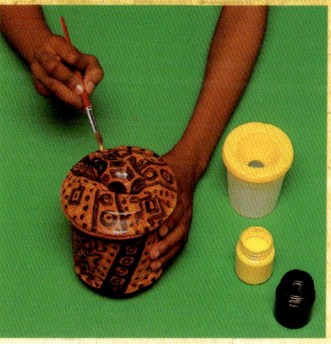

7 Paint the pot with Aztec designs in black and yellow. When you have finished, varnish the pot with a thin coat of glue to make it shiny.

THE MESOAMERICAN MARKET

Inca Master Masons

THE ROCKS OF THE ANDES MOUNTAINS in Peru provided high quality granite for the Incas, who used them for impressive public buildings. These included temples, fortresses, palaces, holy shrines, and aqueducts (stone channels for carrying water supplies). Most buildings were on a grand scale, but all were of a simple design. Many remain in place to this day.

The mit'a labor system provided the workforce. In the quarries, massive rocks that weighed up to 130 tons were cracked and shifted with stone hammers and bronze crowbars. They were hauled with ropes on log rollers or sleds. On site, the stones were shaped to fit, and rubbed smooth with water and sand. Smaller stone blocks were used for upper walls and lesser buildings.

Incan stonemasons had only basic tools. They used plumblines (weighted cords) to make the walls straight. They had no mortar or cement, but the stones fitted together perfectly.

Bringer of Water
This beautifully engineered stone water channel was built across a valley floor by Incan stonemasons. Aqueducts, often covered, were used both for irrigation and for drinking supplies. Irrigation schemes were being built in Peru as early as around 4,500 years ago.

Building the Temple
These rectangular stone blocks were part of the holiest site in the Inca Empire, the Coricancha (Temple of the Sun). Incan stonework was deliberately designed to withstand the earthquakes that regularly shake the region. The original temple on this site was badly damaged by a tremor in 1650.

An Incan Granary
You will need: ruler, pencil, beige, dark, and cream card, scissors, white pencil, paints, paintbrush, water pot, compass, masking tape, white glue, hay or straw.

1 Use a ruler and pencil to mark eight strips 3½ in. long and ⅛ in. wide, and one strip 14¼ in. long and ⅛ in. wide on beige card. Cut them out.

2 On the dark card, draw a curved shape 13¼ in. along the base, 4¼ in. in height, and 12 in. along the top. Cut it out. Cut out a doorway 2½ in. high.

3 Paint another piece of card a stone color. Allow to dry. Cut it into "blocks" about ¾ in. high. Glue them one by one to the building shape.

HISTORY IN STONE
Stone walls and streets, such as these fine examples still standing in Ollantaytambo, survive to tell a story. Archaeology is much more difficult in the rainforests to the east, where timber structures rot rapidly in the hot, moist air. That is one reason we know more about the way people lived in the Andes than in the Amazon region.

INCAN DESIGN
A building in Machu Picchu is an example of typical Incan design. Stonemasons learned many of their skills from earlier Peruvian civilizations. Openings that are wider at the bottom than the top (trapezoid) are seen only in Incan buildings.

Storehouses were built of neat stone blocks. They kept precious grain dry and secure.

A MASSIVE FORTRESS
Llamas still pass before the mighty walls of Sacsahuaman, at Cuzco. This building was a fortress with towers and terraces. It also served as a royal palace and a sacred shrine. Its multisided boulders are precisely fitted. It is said to have been built over many years by 30,000 laborers. It was one of many public buildings raised in the reign of Pachakuti Inka Yupanki.

4 Use a compass to draw a circle 7 in. across on cream card. Cut it out, and cut out one quarter. Tape the straight cut edges together to form a cone.

5 Make a circle by joining the ends of the 14½ in. strip with masking tape. Then fix the eight 3½ in. strips around the edge and in the middle.

6 Glue short pieces of straw or hay all over the cardboard cone to form the thatched roof of the granary. The thatch should all run in the same direction.

7 Join the edges of the walls with masking tape. Fold in the sides of the doorway. Put the rafters on top. The thatched roof fits over the rafters.

Glossary

A
alloy A mixture of metals melted together to create a new substance.
ancestor A member of the same family who died long ago.
Aztecs Mesoamerican people who lived in northern and central Mexico.

B
barter The exchange of goods, one for another.

C
caste One of four social classes into which Hindus of India were divided.
chinampa An Aztec garden built on the fertile, reclaimed land on the lake shore.
city-state A city, and its surrounding villages, with its own god and ruler.
civil servant Someone who works for the government.
civilization A society that has made advances into the arts, science and technology, law and government.
codex An Aztec folding book.
colony A settlement of people outside their own country. The Greeks founded many colonies around the Mediterranean sea.
cowrie A seashell used as currency near the coastal regions of ancient India.

D
daikon A large, white radish grown in Japan.
delta A coastal region where the river slips into coastal waterways before flowing into the sea.
die A tool for punching a design into metal.
drought A long, dry period without rainfall.
dynasty A period of rule by the same royal family.

E
emperor The ruler of an empire.
empire A large number of different lands ruled over by a single person or government.
excavate To dig in the ground to discover ancient ruins and remains.

F
flax A plant that yields fibers that are woven into a fabric called linen.
flint A hard, flaky stone with sharp edges. It is used to make tools and weapons.

G
gypsum A type of limestone used for sculpture.
guilds Groups of workers who checked quality, trained young people, and looked after old and sick members.

H
hemp A fibrous plant that was often used to make coarse clothes or textiles in China.
hunter-gatherer A person whose way of life involves hunting wild animals and gathering plant foods.

I
irrigate To bring water to dry land.
ivory Elephant tusks used to make furniture, boxes and handles.

L
lapis lazuli A dark blue, semiprecious stone used for jewelry and seals.

M
marl Natural lime, dug from under the ground.
Maya People who lived in southeastern Mexico, Guatemala, and Belize. The Mayan lands were conquered between A.D. 1524–1542.
merchant A person who buys and sells goods for a profit.
metronomi Greek officials whose job it was to stop merchants and traders from cheating each other. They oversaw the weighing out of dry goods.
midden A rubbish tip or dunghill.

millet A type of grain crop.

N
Neolithic (New Stone Age) A period that began about two million years ago when the first stone tools were made.

O
olive The fruit of the olive tree. An important crop in ancient Greece, olives were eaten as an appetizer and pressed to make olive oil.
oppida The Roman name for Celtic towns.

P
peasant A poor country dweller.
pharaoh The ruler of ancient Egypt.
plateau High, flat land, usually among mountains.
plumbline A weighted cord, held up to see if a wall, or other construction, is vertical.
porcelain The finest quality of pottery. It is made from kaolin clay and is fired at a high temperature.
potcheca Aztec merchants.
prehistoric Belonging to the time before written records were made.
priest Someone who offered prayers and sacrifices on behalf of worshippers at a temple.

Q
quern A hand-mill used for grinding corn.

S
scribe A professional writer, a clerk, or civil servant.
serfs People who are not free to move from the land they farm without the permission of their landlord.
shaduf A bucket on a weighted pole, used by the Egyptians to move water from the river Nile into the fields on the banks.
sickle A tool with a curved blade used to harvest crops.
Silk Road The overland trading route that stretched from northern China, through Asia to Europe.
silt Fine grains of soil found at the bottom of rivers and lakes.
slaves People who were owned by their masters as opposed to being free.
survey To measure land or buildings. Land is surveyed before the construction of a building or road or any other structure.

T
tanbo Flooded fields where rice was grown.
tax Goods, money or services paid to the government.
temple A special buiding where a god or goddess is worshipped.
textile Cloth produced by weaving threads together.
threshing To beat or thrash out grain from the corn.
tribute Goods given by a country to its conquerors, as a mark of submission.

U
uictli A Mesamerican digging stick that is used like a spade.

V
vallus The Roman name for a Celtic farm machine, used for reaping (cutting) grain crops.
Viking Scandinavian peoples who lived by sea raiding in the early Middle Ages.

W
wampum Shells, or beads made from shells, strung together and used as currency and to record historical events.
winnow To sift the grain, from the (chaff) husks of the corn.

Y
yoke A long piece of wood or bamboo, used to help carry heavy loads. The yoke was placed across the shoulder, and a load was hung from each end to balance it.

Glossary

Index

A
alcohol 55
amber 50
amphorae 43
animals 4, 10-11, 18, 26, 38, 39, 46-7
aqueducts 60
Arctic 13, 54-5
art 6, 7, 42-3
axes 12, 13
Aztec 56-9

B
banking 14
barley 8, 9, 18, 19, 46, 47
bartering 6, 12-13, 22, 32, 30, 58
Buddhism 34
building 5, 6, 60-1
business 6, 14-15

C
caravans 14, 33
carpenters 21
carpets 35
cattle 4, 10-11, 18-19, 27, 39, 46
Celts 46-9
China 5, 24-31
cloth 28, 34-5
civil service 46, 47
cocoa 57
coins 5, 6, 30, 32-3, 40, 42, 44, 48, 50
Confucius 24, 25
craftspeople 5, 6, 20-1, 36, 38, 42-3
crops 4, 8-9, 18, 19, 26-7, 46, 47, 56

D
Deir el-Medina 20-1
Demeter, goddess of grain 39
diseases 54
dogs 11
donkeys 14, 41
dragons 29

E
Egypt 5, 6, 16-23
exotic goods 15, 22-3, 32, 33, 51

F
fertilizers 46
fields 46
fishing 38
floating gardens 57
flour 9, 17
fortresses 61
fruit 18, 19
fur trading 12, 52, 53, 54

G
gardens 57
geese 47
goats 4, 10, 11
gold 20, 22, 23, 30, 48
Greece 5, 38-43

H
herders 10-11, 19
Hinduism 34
horses 4, 10, 41
hunter-gatherers 4, 12

I
Inca Empire 60-1
India 32-5
irrigation 4, 9, 18, 19, 25, 60

J
Japan 36-7
jewelry 15, 20, 42, 43

K
Kanesh 14

L
land reclamation 56-7
llamas 11
longhouses 8

M
maize (corn) 4, 6, 7, 56, 58
markets 6, 30, 31, 41, 44, 58
masons 21, 60
Maya 56-7, 58-9
merchants 36, 24-5, 41, 50-1, 58-9
Mesopotamia 6, 7, 14-15
millet 26
money 4, 5, 32-3, 30

N
Nile, river 18-19, 16
North American Indians 52-3

O
oats 46
olives 38
oppida (towns) 48-9

P
peasant farmers 4, 5, 17, 24-5, 36-7
Persia 34
pharaohs 16, 17, 22, 23
pigs 10, 26, 46
plows 5, 16, 26, 27, 38, 39, 46
Poseidon, sea god 40
pottery 21, 22, 25, 43, 58
printing on fabric 34-5
Punt 22, 23

Q
Qin Shi Huangdi 6, 30
querns 9, 17

R
rice 5, 8, 9, 26-7, 36
ridges and furrows 47
riding 41
Roman Empire 44-5

S
sandalwood 33
scrimshaw 55
sea travel 40-1
serfs 16-17
shaduf (watering machine) 5, 18-19
sheep 4, 10, 11, 46, 47
shell money 12, 32, 52, 53
ships, merchant 33, 40-1
shops 44
silk 6, 28-9, 34
Silk Road 30, 31, 32, 51
silver 14, 15, 30, 32, 48
skilled workers 20-1, 24
skin trade 13, 54-5, 58
slash and burn 56, 57
slaves 5, 16-17
snacks 39
social status 24, 25
spices 32, 33
stone 12, 60-1
Stone Age 8-13
Sumo wrestlers 36

T
taxes 14, 16, 17, 36, 58
tea 26, 30
temples 60
terracing 9, 36, 57
textiles 6, 34-5
threshing 37
tools 4, 8, 18, 26, 46, 56, 21, 12-13, 55
towns 5, 48-9
trading posts 52-3, 54
trade routes 14, 48-51
trapping 13, 54-5
trophies 14

V
vegetables 18, 19
vegetarians 57
Vikings 50-1

W
wampum belts 52, 53
water 4, 9, 18, 19, 60, 25
wealth 25
weapons 55
whaling 7, 54
wheat 8, 9, 18, 19, 26, 46, 47
wine 48, 50
women 6, 17, 28, 58, 59
woods 22
wool 27

Y
Yacatecuhtli, merchant god 58
Yum Caax, corn god 56